VEGAN AIR COOKBOOK

100+ Super Easy Low-Calorie High Protein Plant-Based Recipes to Air Fry, Grill, Roast and Bake in **Max 45 Minutes**

WRITTEN BY
MARION BARTOLINI

Copyright 2021 © [Marion Bartolini] - All rights reserved. No part of this guide may be reproduced in any form without permission in writing from the publisher except in the case of brief quotations embodied in critical articles or reviews.

Legal & Disclaimer

The information contained in this book and its contents is not designed to replace or take the place of any form of medical or professional advice; and is not meant to replace the need for independent medical, financial, legal or other professional advice or services, as may be required. The content and information in this book have been provided for educational and entertainment purposes only.

The content and information contained in this book have been compiled from sources deemed reliable, and it is accurate to the best of the Author's knowledge, information, and belief. However, the author cannot guarantee its accuracy and validity and cannot be held liable for any errors and/or omissions. Further, changes are periodically made to this book as and when needed. Where appropriate and/or necessary, you must consult a professional (including but not limited to your doctor, attorney, financial advisor or such other professional advisor) before using any of the suggested remedies, techniques, or information in this book.

Upon using the contents and information contained in this book, you agree to hold harmless the Author from and against any damages, costs, and expenses, including any legal fees potentially resulting from the application of any of the information provided by this book. This disclaimer applies to any loss, damages or injury caused by the use and application, whether directly or indirectly, of any advice or information presented, whether for breach of contract, tort, negligence, personal injury, criminal intent, or under any other cause of action.

You agree to accept all risks of using the information presented inside this book.

You agree that by continuing to read this book, where appropriate and/or necessary, you shall consult a professional (including but not limited to your doctor, attorney, or financial advisor or such other advisor as needed) before using any of the suggested remedies, techniques, or information in this book.

To my family

Especially to my children, my mother and all the other people that want to contribute to a more sustainable world.

Contents

VEGAN AIR FRYER COOKBOOK 1
    Rainbow vegetable fritters 8

Introduction 9

Eating Healthy 13

Cooking Tips for Beans, Legumes, and Grains 16
    Why using an Air fryer for cooking Vegan dishes? 17

What are the benefits of an Air Fryer 18

Any tips on using Air Fryer? 20
    These are the top 10 tips on Using Air Fryer 21

Breakfast 23
    Greek Veggie Mix 24
    Tofu Casserole 25
    Greek Veggie with Thyme 26
    Veggie Casserole with Cashew 27
    Easy Breakfast Oats 28
    Pear Vanilla Oatmeal 29
    Pumpkin Oatmeal 30
    Veggie Burrito with Tofu 31
    Apple Steel Cut Oats 32
    Lemony Tofu Casserole 33
    Carrot Mix 34
    Blueberries Vanilla Oats 35
    Apple and Pears Mix 36
    Bell Pepper and Beans Oatmeal 37
    Banana and Walnuts Oats 38
    Cinnamon Granola 39
    Zucchini Oatmeal 40
    Almond and Cranberry Quinoa 41

Sweet Quinoa Mix 42

Brunch 43
Couscous and black bean bowl 44
Spicy cauliflower rice 45
Radish hash browns 46

Lunch 47
Air fried brussels sprouts 48
Easy rosemary green beans 49
Garlic eggplant slices 50
Lemony falafel 51
Sweet and sour tofu 52
Crispy chickpeas 53
Skinny pumpkin chips 54
Rainbow vegetable fritters 55
Mediterranean vegetable skewers 56
Fried peppers with sriracha mayo 57
Balsamic root vegetables 58
Tofu nuggets with ginger soy marinade 59
Thai veggie bites 60
Coconut French toast 61
Beignets 62
Potato wedges in cashew sauce 63
Fruit crumble 64
Cajun French fry sandwich with mushroom gravy 65
Vegan French toast 66

Dinner 67
Flavorsome bitter gourd 68
Spinach with groundnuts 69
Flavorsome and fiery aubergine 70
Tofu with peanut dipping sauce 71
Brown rice, spinach and tofu frittata 72
Coconut curry vegetable rice bowls 73
Tofu with Sticky Orange Sauce 74

Side Dish Recipes 75
    Batter-fried scallions 76
    Beets and carrots 77
    Broccoli crisps 78
    Mayo brussels sprouts 79
    Green beans and shallots 80
    Herbed roasted potatoes 81
    Easy frizzled leeks 82

Fruit and Vegetables 83
    Toasty pepper bites 84
    Platter of brussels and pine nuts 85
    Crispy roasted broccoli 86
    Cinnamon butternut squash fries 87
    Cheesy artichokes 88
    Paprika tomatoes 89
    Avocado and tomato salad 90
    Sesame broccoli mix 91
    Cabbage sauté 92
    Tomatoes and kidney beans 93
    Glazed mushrooms 94
    Garlic corn 95

Pasta & Rice 96
    Pesto Farfalle with Cherry Tomatoes 97
    Lemony Parmesan Risotto with Peas 98
    Rice Bowl with Raisins and Almonds 99
    Vegetable Basmati Rice 100
    Stick of Butter Rice 101
    Jasmine Rice with Cauliflower and Pineapple 102

Bread 103
    Sunflower seeds bread 104
    Baguette bread 105

Dessert 106
    Grilled spiced fruit 107

Caramelized peaches with blueberries	108
Stuffed apples	109
Apple peach crisp	110
Lentils and dates brownies with Stevia and banana flavor	111
Walnut and raisin stuffed apples	112
stevia and peanut butter banana toast	113
Banana s'mores	114
Easy cinnamon twists	115
Orange Cake	116
Tahini oatmeal chocolate chunk cookies	117
Chocolate banana packets	118
Granola cookies	119
Figs and coconut butter mix	120
Cinnamon Toast	121
Apple Dumplings	122
Cocoa and Almonds Bars	123
Cashew Bars	124

RAINBOW VEGETABLE FRITTERS

10 minutes | 12 minutes | Lunch | 02 Servings

INGREDIENTS

- 1 zucchini, grated and squeezed
- 1 cup corn kernels
- 1/2 cup canned green peas
- 4 tablespoons all-purpose flour
- 2 tablespoons fresh shallots, minced
- 1 teaspoon fresh garlic, minced
- 1 tablespoon peanut oil
- Sea salt
- Ground black pepper, to taste
- 1 teaspoon cayenne pepper

COOKING STEPS

1. Combine well all ingredients in a mixing bowl until everything is incorporated.
2. Shape the mixture into patties. Put cooking spray in the air fryer basket.
3. Cook in the preheated air fryer at 365 °F for 6 minutes. Turn and cook the other side for additional 6 minutes.
4. Serve immediately and enjoy!

Nutrition: Calories: 215 Fat: 32g Carbs: 6g Protein: 4g

Introduction

Veganism is fast catching up with many people across the world. The noble idea behind veganism, such as not wanting to exploit the less fortunate animal species of the world by taking what is theirs and selfishly using it for ourselves simply because they do not have the power to stop us, is perhaps, the primary reason for the growth in popularity of this concept.

However, in addition to the above extremely thoughtful reason, the health benefits and other great things about veganism are all sufficiently powerful causes for the expansion of the idea of veganism across the planet. This book is written with an intention to exhort newcomers to try a one-month vegan challenge that has the power to change not just your lifestyle but your entire outlook on life.

Before you decide to try to change your lifestyle to vegan, there are a few things you must know and understand about it. This book aims to do exactly that by giving you a detailed overview in the following areas:

- **what is veganism?**
- **A brief history on veganism**
- **How is veganism useful to you?**
- **Meal plans for a one-month challenge along with recipe outlines**
- **How to stay committed to the cause?**

What is veganism?

You know who vegetarians are? They do not consume poultry, meat, or fish in their diet. Vegans, additionally, do not consume or use any animal products and/or by-products such as dairy products, honey, eggs, leather, silk, fur, and soaps and cosmetics made from animal sources. Vegans are the superset of vegetarians. All vegans are also vegetarians but all vegetarians need not be vegans.

Vegans believe that veganism is not just about their diet but a way of life. As far as possible, vegans avoid exploitation of animals in any form including but not limited to food, clothing, or other purposes. They also avoid items that have been tested on animals before being commercialized. And believe it or not, there is a vegan diet for all kinds of diets ranging from the junk food lovers to the raw food lovers and those in between, too.

History of Veganism

Veganism, although not known as veganism, has been around for many centuries. Examples of prevention of exploitation against and cruelty to animals have been written in history books. Lord Buddha of India and Pythagoras both advocated this concept and had put in rules to ensure their followers ate only plant-based food and completely avoided meats and animal products.

The earliest modern-day veganism is known to have occurred around 1806 CE. During that time, the great English poet P. B. Shelley and Dr. William Lambe publicly objected to consuming dairy products and eggs by humans on ethical grounds. This incident seems to have laid the foundation for modern-day veganism.

In November 1944, six non-dairy vegetarians including Donald Watson and Elsie Shrigley met together and discussed the topic on non-dairy vegetarians' lifestyles and diets. Despite strong opposition, these six members founded the new movement and became actively involved in this new project.

This book deals only with the dietary aspect of veganism, giving you ample sufficient reasons to shift your lifestyle to this healthy and noble one. While the benefits of turning vegan are discussed in another chapter, the kind of foods that you can include in your diet while keeping your energy levels and health not just unchanged but also improved than earlier is huge.

Here is a small list of foods that are known to be totally vegan:

- All kinds of grains and cereals
- All kinds of beans and legumes
- All fruits and vegetables

Other vegan foods include soy milk, vegan mayonnaise, vegan ice cream and cheese, vegan hot dogs, and more. Moreover, a lot of companies have come out with mock meats that give vegans a sense of eating meat. This book also has four chapters dedicated to making vegan foods, which includes easy-to-make recipes.

Why Go Vegan?

Most people in the world want to do the following things by some means or the other:

- Lose weight
- Eat better
- Get fitter and healthier
- Do something for society and the world at large

The great news is that if you shift to a vegan diet, you can achieve all the above goals. And let me assure you, you will enjoy delicious, wholesome, and satiating meals as well.

No loss or reduction in energy levels – There is a misconception that changing to a vegan diet reduces your energy levels. There are numerous unworthy talks of vegans living only on water and a few greens and hence their energy levels have taken a huge dip. And on the other side of the spectrum, there are plenty of spurious rumors that say going vegan is helping them do impossible things. These other-end-of-the-spectrum talks make out vegans to be people who can walk on water! Let me assure you that neither of the extremes is true or based on any scientific studies.

Health benefits are huge when you choose to go vegan. Of course, the initial learning curve is going to be steep and you would have to counter multiple challenges. However, once you have overcome these tough phases and complete the 30-day challenge, you are going feel to happier, lighter, and fit. Moreover, there are multiple studies done by various organizations including the British Dietetic Association that has proven the excellent efficacies of getting fitter and healthier by following a vegan diet.

Here is the list of a few magic foods that can restore energy instantaneously:

Bananas – Already beautifully and naturally packaged by nature, this wonderful tropical fruit is normally the first you must reach out for when you feel tired or fatigued.

Walnuts – Another great pick-me-up tree nut, walnuts are rich in plant proteins, omega fatty acids, and vitamins giving you the almost-instant energy boost.

Green smoothies – Delicious smoothies made by tossing together strawberries, bananas, and orange juices are great and extremely healthy pick-me-ups to fight fatigue.

Coconut water – This is nature's energy drink and is amazingly refreshing and is filled with vitamins and potassium.

Kiwi – This low-fat delicious fruit is an instant energy enhancer triggered by the simple sugars present in it.

Why I chose to mention vegan energy boosters in the beginning itself is to help you overcome doubts regarding your ability to get on with your daily schedule if you choose to go vegan. Today there are many sportspeople who have shifted to this diet to keep fitter and sustain energy levels. So, if highly active people in the field of sports can take advantage of veganism, it should not be difficult for moderately active people like us to take this 30-day challenge and come out with flying colors.

Other great reasons to take the one-month challenge to go vegan are:

Lose weight and yet remain energized – Many of us would love to find a sensible way to lose excess weight and yet remain healthy and fit. Average vegans are known to weigh 20 pounds lesser than average meat-eaters. Despite this, vegan diets do not starve you and make you feel enervated like the usual run-of-the-meal fad diets do.

Keep diseases and health disorders away – The Academy of Nutrition and Dietetics have conducted multiple studies which show that taking the vegan route helps you steer clear of common disorders such as diabetes, hypertension or high blood pressure thereby preventing the onset of many modern-day diseases such as heart attacks, kidney failure, and others.

Vegan foods are yummy and delicious – If you thought going vegan means you would have to give up your favorite ice creams, hamburgers, and chicken sandwiches, then you are wrong. With demand for vegan products soaring, many companies are coming up with amazingly delicious vegan options that taste very much like the non-vegetarian stuff. You will not miss any of the meats and animal products at all. There are plenty of established brands that cater to veganism and deliver really tasty dairy and meat substitutes.

Vegan diets are full of highly nutritious and healthy food items including whole grains, beans and legumes, nuts, soy products, and fresh fruits and vegetables. Here are some of the health benefits that these fiber-rich and healthy food sources provide you with:

- **Minimal saturated fats** – Meats and dairy products contain plenty of saturated fats thereby increasing the risk of cardiovascular diseases. Vegan diets automatically reduce intake of saturated fats enhancing your health condition
- **Fiber** – A vegan diet is high in fiber content that is very conducive to healthy bowel movements.
- **Magnesium** – Dark, green leafy vegetables are a rich source of magnesium, a key element that aids the body in the absorption of calcium.
- **Potassium** – Similarly, potassium, an important mineral that balances acidity and water in our body and helps in the removal of toxins, is found plenty in plant-based foods.
- **Proteins** – Meat-eaters invariably end up with more proteins than is needed by the body. Vegan diets, which include nuts, beans, and legumes, have the right amount of proteins for us.

Vegan diets provide other critically essential nutrients such as Vitamins E and C, phytochemicals, antioxidants, and foliate. These help in keeping your immunity system healthy and robust, and also prevent age-related diseases such as Alzheimer's and Parkinson's disease and keep your overall body organs functioning well.

Vegan diets have the power to prevent the following diseases that are very common in today's high-stress unhealthy lifestyle:

- Cardiovascular diseases
- Reduced cholesterol due to the complete absence of meat and dairy products in your diet
- Age-related macular degeneration
- Reduced risk of breast cancer
- Reduced risk of contracting ailments like diabetes, hypertension, cataracts, colon and prostate cancer, arthritis, and osteoporosis

In addition to improved health and prevention of diseases, going vegan makes you stronger, more energetic, and more attractive. Here is how:

Lowered Body Mass Index – Cutting meat and dairy out of your diet naturally reduces Body Mass Index.

Weight loss – Weight loss is an unquestioned effect of a vegan diet.

Healthy skin – Consuming rich sources of Vitamins A and E from nuts and fruits and vegetables enhance the texture and health of your skin.

Reduced allergy symptoms – Plant-based foods do not trigger as many allergic reactions in humans as dairy and meat products do.

Less intake of mercury – A lot of shellfish and fish contain high levels of mercury, which we take in when we eat these foods. Switching to veganism does away with this toxin completely.

The above are only some of the great reasons that you must start off this 30-day vegan challenge. Instead of finding reasons not to do something good, focus on the above reasons which tell you why you should do it and dive straight in. Summon some extra willpower and after you complete this challenge you can rest assured that the willpower would come on its own when you see and feel the wondrous new VEGAN YOU.

Eating Healthy

If you haven't already been tracking your "macros and micros" for your regular vegan diet, it's about time that you started. There is no better way to make sure you're getting the exact amount of calories, and the exact amount of nutrients, that your body needs without tracking your macros and micros. "Macros" is an abbreviation that stands for "macronutrients," and they're what the Keto diet is based on. The three main macronutrients required for human life are carbohydrates, proteins, and fats. That's right! Tracking your macronutrients is just as easy as tracking how many grams of protein, carbohydrates, and fats you're eating in each meal. It does get a bit more complicated than that, but it's nothing you won't be able to handle. "Micros," then, stands for "micronutrients," and these are quite different from what you might be thinking. Micronutrients are actually the vitamins and minerals that your body requires to function, and micros are often essential for macros to do their jobs. Without the help of certain minerals, our macronutrients wouldn't be able to synthesize new proteins, add in our cellular regeneration, and help move bad molecules like harmful cholesterol out of our arteries. In order to make sure you're getting your proper dosages of micronutrients, you take supplements! One of the many helpful connections between veganism and the Keto diet is that both tend to require a healthy amount of added vitamins and minerals. However, it's worth noting that there are many more suggested micronutrients that we're supposed to get per day beyond just the popular five or seven. In fact, there are a whopping twenty-five micronutrients that our diets are supposed to provide us with every day. Although some of the amounts are so small, they're measured in micrograms—it's worth taking a look at this list to know what else you might want to supplement.

A multivitamin in combination with your regular vegan diet supplements should supply you with the perfect amount of each of these smaller micronutrients. You should, however, consult your physician before you start taking iron supplements. Tracking your macronutrients is definitely more involved, but there's a special tool that we're going to borrow from the body-building community to make it easier.

How Weighing Your Portions Ensures Success:

Nobody likes a scale, but isn't it true that everything's better when there's food involved? Back when the fitness community began to really focus on how our diets were facilitating weight loss, many body-builders and intense athletes started to use food scales as a way to be more precise about the portion sizes. But not just portions of whole meals—weighing your food with a food scale allows you to calculate the number of macronutrients and the number of calories in each portion of the meals you're going to prepare each week. The first step to using your food scale is to download an app called My Fitness Pal (the most popular macronutrient tracking app out there, and a great community to get involved with if you're vegan!). If you don't have a smartphone, feel free to use an online calculator—you'll be able to find more than a few. The next step is to visit your local restaurant supply store to stock up on large containers. Each week, when you prepare your meal on Sunday, you'll want to use your food scale to weight the entire cooked meal (all three or four portions together). To do this, set your chosen container on your scale and make the numbers read "00.00" – you're going to be pouring your entire meal into these containers to measure, so bigger is better. Once you've measured the full meal, use your application to plug in each of the ingredients you used in the meal and their amounts. This is just another reason that it's important to be organized with your grocery shopping. The resulting numbers should give you the number of total calories and nutrients, and if you divide by the number of portions you intend for the meal to make, you'll have an accurate nutritional label of calories, vitamins, and nutrients.

Prepare to Meal Prep:

Meal prep, short for meal preparation, is a technique known far and wide in the fitness community as one of the best ways to ensure that you're eating a protein-packed, well-balanced meal with the proper portions to maximize your weight loss (or gain) without taking up too much time. During the week, most of us work forty hours or more—and if you're adding in the time that it takes to go to the gym, commute back and forth, finish your weekly work, and manage whatever other responsibilities you have—there isn't much time left for home-cooking. However, the meals you might purchase at a supermarket or restaurant simply won't fit in with a strict diet, especially one that combines two strict methods of eating. Meal prep is a great technique for busy individuals to use to make sure that they're getting the proper amount of fats, proteins, and carbohydrates for their diet and fitness. When you're eating a vegan Keto diet, you want to pay extra attention to the breakdown of nutrients in your food (and how those nutrients measure up in terms of carbohydrate content). Skip down to the section titled "Meal Prep Tips for Vegans Eating Keto" to get a better handle on your nutrient breakdown if you're already familiar with how to meal prep. If you aren't, everything you need to know is right below.

How to Meal Prep:

The idea behind meal prepping is incredibly simple, but the timing is a little less self-explanatory. Meal prepping is a practice that takes place normally on a Sunday before the work week begins when most people have enough time to cook multiple large-batch meals in one day. Yes, you'll most likely end up cooking more meals on Sunday than you'll get to eat. It's alright. You'll thank yourself late in the week. Meal prepping on Sundays normally starts with a trip to the grocery store to make sure your produce is as fresh as possible. While some more advanced meal prep specialists have adapted to using their freezer for fresh ingredients, you'll only want to rely on your freezer for full meals at the beginning of your journey. Normally meal prep consists of all the dinner, lunches, breakfasts, and snacks you can possibly prepare to give yourself time to go to the gym and get enough sleep while you're working. The easiest way to tackle meal prep for the first time is to start by making four lunches and four dinners in one Sunday. Although that might seem like a fair amount, it's really only two meals that you'll be cooking in large batches. Meal prep is known for creating quite the large mess in the kitchen, so take the time to do a bit of pre-cleaning so that you won't regret it afterward. A pre-clean is a great time to make sure all your largest pots, saucepans, and skillets and ready to cook with; one meal might not always mean one pot. Many vegan Keto recipes rely on sautéing, steaming, and grilling in order to give a smoky depth of flavor to foods with a more neutral palette. While your gathering your cooking utensils, remember that meal prepping is all about organization. Before you go to the grocery store, make sure you have all your ingredients written down and that you know what to look for when it comes to labels. High carb content in both carbs and net carbs will impact your ability to reach Ketosis. Once you're ready to start cooking, make sure you have plenty of healthy cooking oils on hand to lubricate your pans. Coconut oil is recommended, but with its low smoke point, you're welcome to use olive oil if you need to cook hotter for longer. After you're finished, it's crucial that you have equal sized Tupperware for proper storage. Nothing ruins a good middle of the week meal like opening your squash spaghetti to freezer burn. Most cooked meals take three to five days to go bad, so while you don't have to put your prepped meals in the freezer, sometimes it's a good back up if your fridge is low on space. That's about all there is to the process of preparing your meals, but what about prepping meals specifically for a vegan Keto diet? Does anything change?

Cooking Tips for Beans, Legumes, and Grains

1. Soak beans for at least 8 to 10 hours (preferably overnight) to remove any anti-nutrients. This reduces the chances of stomach cramps, gas, and bloating.
2. If you're pressed for time, you can also use a quick Soak Method. Just boil enough water to cover the beans, add in the beans, let simmer for 10 minutes, and set aside for an hour.
3. Soak quinoa and brown rice for a couple of hours. Lentils and other grains don't require any prior soaking.

Cooking utensils

1. Cooking in a pressure cooker

Drain the water from one cup of previously soaked beans, grains, or lentils. Rinse the vegetables well and add them to a 6-to 8-quart cooker.

Add 2-4 cups of water. Close the lid and cook on high heat.

When the cooker reaches a high pressure, lower the heat, and cook for an extra 7-10 minutes. Turn off the heat, let everything cool, and open the lid.

2. Cooking in a slow cooker

Drain the water from one cup of previously soaked beans/quinoa/brown rice, rinse well, and add to a smaller slow cooker.

Pour in 2-4 cups of water. Add other ingredients except for salt (for stews, soups, and one pot meals). Cover the slow cooker with a lid and cook on high heat for 3-4 hours, or 7-8 hours on low heat. Add in salt in the last 10 minutes of cooking.

3. Cooking Grains and Lentils on a Stovetop

Respect the following quantities when cooking on a stove top. Water and Yield are measured in cups, and time in minutes.

WHY USING AN AIR FRYER FOR COOKING VEGAN DISHES?

If you already own (or you are thinking of buying) an Air Fryer you will have in your hands all the tools that will guarantee you top results. You can use your Air Fryer to cook all your vegan dishes from this cookbook in a quick and easy way, without compromising on taste and while staying within budget!

As you might already know, an air fryer is a small type of oven. It is an innovative countertop kitchen gadget that fries or cook's food by circulating hot air via convection current. The air fryer has a heating ring that produces hot air. There is also a mechanical fan that circulates the hot air all over the food at high speed. This hot air cook or fries the food to give the same crispy product as the oil fried variety. The difference between air frying and oil frying is that while oil frying involves immersion of the food into the hot oil to cook, the air fryer doesn't. It means that you can achieve the same cooking results as in oil frying but with little to no oil.

The air fryer works great for foods like roasted vegetables, especially roasted garlic, vegetables, grains, pulses and tofu. Most air fryers come with timers and temperature adjustments to make for more precise cooking. There is an opening at the top that takes in air, heated up by the heating rings, and subsequently blown over the food, thereby efficiently cooking them. A cooking basket also sits on top of a drip tray inside which the food is cooked. This basket needs to be shaken frequently to ensure even mixing of oil and a better cooking result. While most models have agitators that initiate this shaking at regular intervals, most others do not, and the shaking should be done manually.

Since air fryers don't require as much oil as oil frying does, they are generally considered healthier. An air fryer reduces the oil content of food to nearly 80% less than oil frying. It is because the food does not absorb as much oil as with oil frying. However, this difference has led to arguments about the taste of air fried food compared to the oil fried variety. Since oil adds more flavor to fried food as it is being absorbed, it comes as no surprise if an air fried food tastes slightly different from oil fried ones. An excellent example is French fries that may taste a lot different when air fried than the usual oil fried delicacy. Tofu, however, turns out pretty great whether sprinkled with oil or not before air frying.

Moreover, spraying the food with oil before air frying gives it an added crispiness compared to the one that was not sprinkled before air frying. Oil on its own is also one of the essential macronutrients and will come in handy in the right proportion.

There are many heart friendly oils out there, which you can spread over your food before air frying to achieve that fabulous taste. These oils can be used to sprinkle your food before air frying to maintain a healthier diet. Just like most innovative appliances, the air fryer might come with an initial dread on how to use it effectively. Once mastered, the art of air frying is what many people find themselves resorting to more often than not. Even though air frying is a convenient hands-off cooking method, using the air fryer is more than just turning on the device and leaving your kitchen.

What are the benefits of an Air Fryer

As you are aware, an air fryer is a great appliance to have in your kitchen. Not only does it save on the time taken to cook, but it also produces healthy meals. It's worthwhile looking at some of the health benefits provided by it.

- Healthy foods

The air fryer is quite popular, owing to producing healthy meals. It reduces oils and fats, thereby making the result relatively healthy. The same cannot be said about standard cooking techniques where you must add in lots of oils and fats. These can adversely affect your health and be the reason for obesity and illnesses. Therefore, an air fryer is best suited for improving their health by making changes in their cooking habits.

- Time

The time crunch is one of the most significant issues people face today and age, as everybody is preoccupied with one thing or another. The air fryer effectively solves this problem, as you can prepare foods within a short period. It works by cutting down on 20% of the time taken to cook foods the traditional way. This feature comes in handy for many people, including working professionals, students, and the elderly. If you are always short of time, then it is best to invest in an air fryer as soon as you get a chance.

- ## Usage

The air fryer is extremely easy to use and can be used by just about anyone. The machine is supplied with a manual that can be used to operate the appliance. The manual will also provide you with the right temperatures and times to cook different meals. With time, you will know the exact measures and be able to cook meals much faster. However, it will take a certain level of trial and error to stumble upon the right temperatures and times until you get used to using it. Remember, your ideas center around traditional cooking.

- ## Effort required

The air fryer is designed to be a very efficient machine that pretty much works by itself. It means that you don't have to put in too much effort to operate it. You just have to prepare the ingredients and add them to the appliance, and it will take it from there. You don't have to sauté, season, cover or keep an eye on the foods you place into the oven. All these steps are eliminated, thereby reducing both your effort and time taken to cook a meal. It makes it ideal for all those who are usually too lazy to cook up a meal and prefer takeout.

- ## Nutritional content

An air fryer helps maintain food's nutritional value. Cooking foods at higher temperatures can cause nutritional value to deplete. This issue is solved with an air fryer as it retains the nutritional content of foods placed into it.

- ## Cost of cooking

The air fryer helps in cutting down on the overall costs of cooking. It cuts down on the use of oils and fats, thereby reducing the overall costs of providing your family with food. Another advantage of cooking with an air fryer is that it tends to expand the food item, thereby decreasing the quantity required to cook a meal, reducing cooking costs. You will be surprised by the reduction in your budget and overall cooking costs.

- **Variety in cooking**

Throwing parties and cooking big meals will now be quite easy thanks to the air fryer's multitasking ability. One of the most advantages of using an air fryer is that it can be used for many different cooking purposes. Right from roasting to frying to baking, the air fryer can be put to many uses. You can also use it to grill foods, making it a truly versatile appliance to have in your kitchen. What's more, you will have the choice of cooking several dishes at the same time by using the separator provided with the fryer.

- **Maintaining the fryer**

It is easy to maintain the air fryer, as you do not have to do too much to stay clean. You can eliminate the need to clean several appliances and get away with cleaning, just one that servings many purposes. The machine is easy to clean from the outside. The basket and catching utensil are dishwasher friendly.

- **Cost saving**

The air fryer is quite cheap, price wise, considering the utility that it can provide. You don't need to buy different appliances like an oven, a grill, a chip fryer, etc. It can be done through the air fryer alone. Think of it as a onetime investment that is sure to last you a lifetime if taken care of following manufacturer instructions. Always read these, as the maintenance of each fryer will differ.

These descriptions show the different benefits of using air fryer. Each one of these contributes towards making it an ideal appliance to have in your kitchen.

Any tips on using Air Fryer?

An air fryer is a little device that has rapidly grown in popularity in the last few years. It is supposed to help you bake food. Some people call them air fryer ovens. You may remember when you saw your first Indian dish inspired by food fried in oil. Now, it's time to take you on a tour of the world and in a healthier way!

In the last few years, air fryers have become more and more popular. A lot of websites and blogs are now making them out to be the new microwave oven or rice cooker. The fine folks at Amana, pioneers in air fryers, sent me one of their most hot selling models.

Frying has become a bad word lately. As a result, we try to cut down on it in as many of our recipes as possible. Fortunately, air fryers are a great way to make food taste like it's been fried when it hasn't. So, here are some tips on cooking with air fryers:

Air fryers are available in multiple sizes. Look for one that fits the amount of food you want to make. Some air fryers are small enough that you would only use them for a snack or a single person. Others could make enough food for a whole family. There's also a market for commercial sized air fryers, and they're quite large. They could make enough food for a dozen people easily. They're also versatile in that they can be used for baking and as steamers.

Your new air fryer comes with a lot of accessories. You don't need to worry too much about them at the moment. Here are a few tips.

THESE ARE THE TOP 10 TIPS ON USING AIR FRYER

1. No matter what your air fryer comes with, you'll also need a pan and a spatula. The pan is for use as a defroster and a catch-all for when you take out the food. The spatula is to get food out of the air fryer. Remember that the food comes out very hot, so use caution.

2. Look at the shape of your air fryer. It may be a square or a circle. You can do a lot of things to a square air fryer, but few to a circle one. Look at your recipe and decide what you want to use it for.

3. The air fryer's controls are arguably the most important part. The air fryer has a lot of temperature controls that are quite precise. Unlike a microwave oven, an air fryer can give you a wide range of temperatures. You can cook things at really low temperatures, and you can cook things at incredibly hot temperatures that you couldn't use otherwise. Of course, you can also use it at the default temperature. Use the recommendations for your model in the instruction manual to help figure out which temperature is best for your needs.

4. You can make very unique recipes using the air fryer. The temperature and the food you use set the tone of the meal. The temperature you want to use should depend mostly on the type of food you're making, or even how you want it to come out. Low temperature cooking is helpful when you want to cook things slowly. You also want foods with a lot of moisture to be cooked at a high temperature because they cook through faster. You can make dishes with vegetables and meats evenly. You can also make quick breads since they would take less time and the other ingredients are easier to get.

5. Air fryers are very inexpensive. No matter what your budget is, there is an air fryer that fits it. They're mainly used for snacks. However, you can use the air fryer for other recipes if you want. They're a great alternative to the waffle iron, and you can cook a wide range of foods with them.

6. There are different components to an air fryer, and you can use each of them for different purposes. The top is traditionally used for eggs and for steaming. The middle can be used for both frying foods and steaming them. The bottom is typically for fries and other fried foods.

7. Air fryers are very versatile. It's hard to find a recipe that can't be used in an air fryer. You can even make foods with breading. People can even make grills and pizzas in air fryers.

8. If you're looking for the best air fryer, you can't go wrong with a Norpro. This is a great air fryer that is affordable and very easy to use. It has multiple functions and will work in no time.

9. Most air fryers have a filter. You need to make sure you always keep the filter cleaned. As much as you don't want to clean your air fryer, you have to clean the filter. This is very important because all the cooking oil is retained in the filter.

10. There are different types of air fryers. The ones that are made of glass and stainless steel are the most expensive. They're also more attractive. There are the ones that are made of plastic. Finally, there are the ones that are made from non-stick surfaces. These are the cheapest and also the most commonly sold air fryers.

Now you have in your hands all the information needed to safely proceed toward your Vegan lifelong transformation to increase your Health, your Confidence and your Vitality. Using your Air Fryer will also guarantee you delicious and time effective recipes that will help you integrate the foundational habits of health into your everyday routine. By incorporating the habits of Health into your new lifestyle, you will be able to take your first steps towards the life you wish for. You will feel restored, more confident and your energy levels will be up. Enjoy life to the fullest!

Breakfast

GREEK VEGGIE MIX

10 minutes | **45 minutes** | **Breakfast** | **04 Servings**

INGREDIENTS

- sliced
- 8 ounces zucchini, sliced
- 8 ounces bell peppers, chopped
- 2 garlic cloves, minced
- 5 tablespoons olive oil
- 1 bay leaf
- 1 thyme spring
- 2 onions, chopped
- 8 ounces tomatoes, cut into quarters
- Salt and black pepper to the taste

COOKING STEPS

1. Heat up a pan that fits your air fryer with 2 tablespoons oil over medium-high heat, add eggplant, salt and pepper, stir, cook for 5 minutes and transfer to a bowl.
2. Heat up the pan with 1 more tablespoon oil, add zucchini, cook for 3 minutes and transfer over eggplant pieces.
3. Heat up the pan again, add bell peppers, stir, cook for 2 minutes and pour over the other veggies.
4. Heat up the pan with 2 tablespoons oil, add onions, stir and cook for 3 minutes.
5. Add tomatoes, the rest of the veggies, bay leaf, thyme, garlic, salt and pepper, stir, transfer to your air fryer and cook at 300° f for 30 minutes.
6. Divide between plates and serve for breakfast.
7. Enjoy!

Nutrition: Calories 100 Fat 1g Carb 7g Protein 3g

TOFU CASSEROLE

10 minutes | 20 minutes | Breakfast | 04 Servings

INGREDIENTS

- 1 teaspoon lemon zest, grated
- 14 ounces tofu, cubed
- 1 tablespoon lemon juice
- 2 tablespoons nutritional yeast
- 1 tablespoon apple cider vinegar
- 1 tablespoon olive oil
- 2 garlic cloves, minced
- 10 ounces spinach, torn
- ½ cup yellow onion, chopped
- ½ teaspoon basil, dried
- 8 ounces mushrooms, sliced
- Salt and black pepper to the taste
- ¼ teaspoon red pepper flakes
- Cooking spray

COOKING STEPS

1. Spray your air fryer with some cooking spray, arrange tofu cubes on the bottom, add lemon zest, lemon juice, yeast, vinegar, olive oil, garlic, spinach, onion, basil, mushrooms, salt, pepper and pepper flakes, toss, cover and cook at 365° f for 20 minutes.

2. Divide between plates and serve for breakfast.

3. Enjoy!

Nutrition: Calories 246 Fat 6g Carb 12g Protein 4g

GREEK VEGGIE WITH THYME

10 minutes   **45 minutes**   **Breakfast**   **04 Servings**

INGREDIENTS

- 8 ounces eggplant, sliced
- 8 ounces zucchini, sliced
- 8 ounces bell peppers, chopped
- 2 garlic cloves, minced
- 5 tablespoons olive oil
- 1 bay leaf
- 1 thyme spring
- 2 onions, chopped
- 8 ounces tomatoes, cut into quarters
- Salt and black pepper to the taste

COOKING STEPS

1. Heat up a pan that fits your air fryer with 2 tablespoons oil over medium-high heat, add eggplant, salt and pepper, stir, cook for 5 minutes and transfer to a bowl.
2. Heat up the pan with 1 more tablespoon oil, add zucchini, cook for 3 minutes and transfer over eggplant pieces.
3. Heat up the pan again, add bell peppers, stir, cook for 2 minutes and pour over the other veggies.
4. Heat up the pan with 2 tablespoons oil, add onions, stir and cook for 3 minutes.
5. Add tomatoes, the rest of the veggies, bay leaf, thyme, garlic, salt and pepper, stir, transfer to your air fryer and cook at 300°f for 30 minutes.
6. Divide between plates and serve for breakfast.
7. Enjoy!

Nutrition: Calories 100 Fat 1g Carb 7g Protein 3g

VEGGIE CASSEROLE WITH CASHEW

10 minutes | 16 minutes | Breakfast | 04 Servings

INGREDIENTS

- 2 teaspoons onion powder
- ¾ cup cashews, soaked for 30 minutes and drained
- ¼ cup nutritional yeast
- 1 teaspoon garlic powder
- ½ teaspoon sage, dried
- Salt and black pepper to the taste
- 1 yellow onion, chopped
- 2 tablespoons parsley, chopped
- 3 garlic cloves, minced
- 1 tablespoon olive oil
- 4 red potatoes, cubed
- ½ teaspoon red pepper flakes

COOKING STEPS

1. In your blender, mix cashews with onion powder, garlic powder, nutritional yeast, sage, salt and pepper and pulse really well.
2. Add oil to your air fryer's pan and preheat the machine to 370°f.
3. Arrange potatoes, pepper flakes, garlic, onion, salt, pepper and parsley in the pan,
4. Add cashews sauce, toss, cover and cook for 16 minutes
5. Divide between plates and serve for breakfast.
6. Enjoy!

Nutrition: Calories 218 Fat 6g Carb 14g Protein 5g

EASY BREAKFAST OATS

10 minutes | 15 minutes | Breakfast | 04 Servings

INGREDIENTS

- 2 cups almond milk
- 1 cup steel cut oats
- 2 cups water
- 1/3 cup cherries, dried
- 2 tablespoons cocoa powder
- ¼ cup stevia
- ½ teaspoon almond extract
- For the sauce:
- 2 tablespoons water
- 1 and ½ cups cherries
- ¼ teaspoon almond extract

COOKING STEPS

1. In your air fryer's pan, mix almond milk with oats, water, dried cherries, cocoa powder, stevia and ½ teaspoon almond extract, stir, cover and cook at 360°f for 15 minutes.

2. Meanwhile, in a small pot, mix 2 tablespoons water with 1 and ½ cups cherries and ¼ teaspoon almond extract, stir, bring to a simmer over medium heat and cook for 10 minutes.

3. Divide oats into bowls, drizzle cherry sauce all over and serve for breakfast.

4. Enjoy!

Nutrition: Calories 172 Fat 7g Carb 12g Protein 6g

PEAR VANILLA OATMEAL

10 minutes | 15 minutes | Breakfast | 03 Servings

INGREDIENTS

- 2 cups coconut milk
- ½ cup steel cut oats
- ½ teaspoon vanilla extract
- 1 pear, chopped
- ½ teaspoon maple extract
- 1 tablespoon stevia

COOKING STEPS

1. In your air fryer's pan, mix coconut milk with oats, vanilla, pear, maple extract and stevia, stir, cover and cook at 360° f for 15 minutes.
2. Divide into bowls and serve for breakfast.
3. Enjoy!

Nutrition: Calories 200 Fat 5g Carb 14g Protein 4g

PUMPKIN OATMEAL

10 minutes | 20 minutes | Breakfast | 04 Servings

INGREDIENTS

- 1 and ½ cups water
- ½ cup pumpkin puree
- 1 teaspoon pumpkin pie spice
- 3 tablespoons stevia
- ½ cup steel cut oats

COOKING STEPS

1. In your air fryer's pan, mix water with oats, pumpkin puree, pumpkin spice and stevia, stir, cover and cook at 360°f for 20 minutes
2. Divide into bowls and serve for breakfast.
3. Enjoy!

Nutrition: Calories 211 Fat 4g Carb 8g Protein 3g

VEGGIE BURRITO WITH TOFU

10 minutes | 15 minutes | Breakfast | 08 Servings

INGREDIENTS

- 16 ounces tofu, crumbled
- 1 green bell pepper, chopped
- ¼ cup scallions, chopped
- 15 ounces canned black beans, drained
- 1 cup vegan salsa
- ½ cup water
- ¼ teaspoon cumin, ground
- ½ teaspoon turmeric powder
- ½ teaspoon smoked paprika
- A pinch of salt and black pepper
- ¼ teaspoon chili powder
- 3 cups spinach leaves, torn
- 8 vegan tortillas for serving

COOKING STEPS

1. In your air fryer, mix tofu with bell pepper, scallions, black beans, salsa, water, cumin, turmeric, paprika, salt, pepper and chili powder, stir, cover and cook at 370°f for 20 minutes

2. Add spinach, toss well, divide this on your vegan tortillas, roll, wrap them and serve for breakfast.

3. Enjoy!

Nutrition: Calories 211 Fat 4g Carb 14g Protein 4g

APPLE STEEL CUT OATS

| 10 minutes | 15 minutes | Breakfast | 06 Servings |

INGREDIENTS

- 1 and ½ cups water
- 1 and ½ cups coconut milk
- 2 apples, cored, peeled and chopped
- 1 cup steel cut oats
- ½ teaspoon cinnamon powder
- ¼ teaspoon nutmeg, ground
- ¼ teaspoon allspice, ground
- ¼ teaspoon ginger powder
- ¼ teaspoon cardamom, ground
- 1 tablespoon flaxseed, ground
- 2 teaspoons vanilla extract
- 2 teaspoons stevia
- Cooking spray

COOKING STEPS

1. Spray your air fryer with cooking spray, add apples, milk, water, cinnamon, oats, allspice, nutmeg, cardamom, ginger, vanilla, flaxseeds and stevia, stir, cover and cook at 360°f for 15 minutes

2. Divide into bowls and serve for breakfast.

3. Enjoy!

Nutrition: Calories 172 Fat 3g Carb 8g Protein 5g

LEMONY TOFU CASSEROLE

10 minutes | 20 minutes | Breakfast | 04 Servings

INGREDIENTS

- 1 teaspoon lemon zest, grated
- 14 ounces tofu, cubed
- 1 tablespoon lemon juice
- 2 tablespoons nutritional yeast
- 1 tablespoon apple cider vinegar
- 1 tablespoon olive oil
- 2 garlic cloves, minced
- 10 ounces spinach, torn
- ½ cup yellow onion, chopped
- ½ teaspoon basil, dried
- 8 ounces mushrooms, sliced
- Salt and black pepper to the taste
- ¼ teaspoon red pepper flakes
- Cooking spray

COOKING STEPS

1. Spray your air fryer with some cooking spray, arrange tofu cubes on the bottom, add lemon zest, lemon juice, yeast, vinegar, olive oil, garlic, spinach, onion, basil, mushrooms, salt, pepper and pepper flakes, toss, cover and cook at 365°f for 20 minutes.

2. Divide between plates and serve for breakfast.

3. Enjoy!

Nutrition: Calories 246 Fat 6g Carb 12g Protein 4g

CARROT MIX

10 minute | **15 minutes** | **Breakfast** | **04 Servings**

INGREDIENTS

- 2 cups coconut milk
- ½ cup steel cut oats
- 1 cup carrots, shredded
- 1 teaspoon cardamom, ground
- ½ teaspoon agave nectar
- A pinch of saffron
- Cooking spray

COOKING STEPS

1. Spray your air fryer with cooking spray, add milk, oats, carrots, cardamom and agave nectar, stir, cover and cook at 365°f for 15 minutes
2. Divide into bowls, sprinkle saffron on top and serve for breakfast.
3. Enjoy!

Nutrition: Calories 202 Fat 7g Carb 8g Protein 3g

BLUEBERRIES VANILLA OATS

10 minutes | 15 minutes | Breakfast | 04 Servings

INGREDIENTS

- 1 cup blueberries
- 1 cup steel cut oats
- 1 cup coconut milk
- 2 tablespoons agave nectar
- ½ teaspoon vanilla extract
- Cooking spray

COOKING STEPS

1. Spray your air fryer with cooking spray, add oats, milk, agave nectar, vanilla and blueberries, toss, cover and cook at 365°f for 10 minutes.
2. Divide into bowls and serve for breakfast.
3. Enjoy!

Nutrition: Calories 202 Fat 6g Carbs 9g Protein 6g

APPLE AND PEARS MIX

10 minutes | 15 minutes | Breakfast | 06 Servings

INGREDIENTS

- 4 apples, cored, peeled and cut into medium chunks
- 1 teaspoon lemon juice
- 4 pears, cored, peeled and cut into medium chunks
- 5 teaspoons stevia
- 1 teaspoon cinnamon powder
- 1 teaspoon vanilla extract
- ½ teaspoon ginger, ground
- ½ teaspoon cloves, ground
- ½ teaspoon cardamom, ground

COOKING STEPS

1. In your air fryer, mix apples with pears, lemon juice, stevia, cinnamon, vanilla extract, ginger, cloves and cardamom, stir, cover, cook at 360°f for 15 minutes
2. Divide into bowls and serve for breakfast.
3. Enjoy!

Nutrition: Calories; 161 Fat 3g Carb 9g Protein 4g

BELL PEPPER AND BEANS OATMEAL

10 minutes | 15 minutes | Breakfast | 06 Servings

INGREDIENTS

- 1 cup steel cut oats
- 2 tablespoons canned kidney beans, drained
- 2 red bell peppers, chopped
- 4 tablespoons coconut cream
- A pinch of sweet paprika
- Salt and black pepper to the taste
- ¼ teaspoon cumin, ground

COOKING STEPS

1. Heat up your air fryer at 360°f, add oats, beans, bell peppers, coconut cream, paprika, salt, pepper and cumin, stir, cover and cook for 16 minutes.
2. Divide into bowls and serve for breakfast.
3. Enjoy!

Nutrition: Calories 173 Fat 4g Carb 12g Protein 4g

BANANA AND WALNUTS OATS

10 minutes | 15 minutes | Breakfast | 04 Servings

INGREDIENTS

- 1 banana, peeled and mashed
- 1 cup steel cut oats
- 2 cups almond milk
- 2 cups water
- ¼ cup walnuts, chopped
- 2 tablespoons flaxseed meal
- 2 teaspoons cinnamon powder
- 1 teaspoon vanilla extract
- ½ teaspoon nutmeg, ground

COOKING STEPS

1. In your air fryer mix oats with almond milk, water, walnuts, flaxseed meal, cinnamon, vanilla and nutmeg, stir, cover and cook at 360°f for 15 minutes.
2. Divide into bowls and serve for breakfast.
3. Enjoy!

Nutrition: Calories 181 Fat 7g Carbs 12g Protein 11g

CINNAMON GRANOLA

10 minutes | 15 minutes | Breakfast | 03 Servings

INGREDIENTS

- ½ cup granola
- ½ cup bran flakes
- 2 green apples, cored, peeled and roughly chopped
- ¼ cup apple juice
- 1/8 cup maple syrup
- 2 tablespoons cashew butter
- 1 teaspoon cinnamon powder
- ½ teaspoon nutmeg, ground

COOKING STEPS

1. In your air fryer, mix granola with bran flakes, apples, apple juice, maple syrup, cashew butter, cinnamon and nutmeg, toss, cover and cook at 365°f for 15 minutes
2. Divide into bowls and serve for breakfast.
3. Enjoy!

Nutrition: Calories 188 Fat 6g Carb 11g Protein 6g

ZUCCHINI OATMEAL

10 minutes | **15 minutes** | **Breakfast** | **04 Servings**

INGREDIENTS

- ½ cup steel cut oats
- 1 carrot, grated
- 1 and ½ cups almond milk
- ¼ zucchini, grated
- ¼ teaspoon nutmeg, ground
- ¼ teaspoon cloves, ground
- ½ teaspoon cinnamon powder
- 2 tablespoons maple syrup
- ¼ cup pecans, chopped
- 1 teaspoon vanilla extract

COOKING STEPS

1. In your air fryer, mix oats with carrot, zucchini, almond milk, cloves, nutmeg, cinnamon, maple syrup, pecans and vanilla extract, stir, cover and cook at 365°f for 15 minutes.
2. Divide into bowls and serve.
3. Enjoy!

Nutrition: Calories 175 Fat 4g Fiber 7g Carbs 12g Protein 7g

ALMOND AND CRANBERRY QUINOA

10 minutes | 15 minutes | Breakfast | 04 Servings

INGREDIENTS

- 1 cup quinoa
- 3 cups coconut water
- 1 teaspoon vanilla extract
- 3 teaspoons stevia
- 1/8 cup coconut flakes
- ¼ cup cranberries, dried
- 1/8 cup almonds, chopped

COOKING STEPS

1. In your air fryer, mix quinoa with coconut water, vanilla, stevia, coconut flakes, almonds and cranberries, toss, cover and cook at 365°f for 13 minutes.

2. Divide into bowls and serve for breakfast.

3. Enjoy!

Nutrition: Calories 146 Fat 5g Carbs 10g Protein 7g

SWEET QUINOA MIX

10 minutes | **14 minutes** | **Breakfast** | **06 Servings**

INGREDIENTS

- ½ cup quinoa
- 1 and ½ cups steel cut oats
- 4 tablespoons stevia
- 4 and ½ cups almond milk
- 2 tablespoons maple syrup
- 1 and ½ teaspoons vanilla extract
- Strawberries, halved for serving
- Cooking spray

COOKING STEPS

1. Spray your air fryer with cooking spray, add oats, quinoa, stevia, almond milk, maple syrup and vanilla extract, toss, cover and cook at 365°f for 14 minutes
2. Divide into bowls, add strawberries on top and serve for breakfast.
3. Enjoy!

Nutrition: Calories 207 Fat 5g Carb 14g Protein 5g

Brunch

Brunch

COUSCOUS AND BLACK BEAN BOWL

10 minutes | 35 minutes | Bread | 04 Servings

INGREDIENTS

- 1 cup couscous
- 1 cup canned black beans, drained and rinsed
- 1 tablespoon fresh cilantro, chopped
- 1 bell pepper, sliced
- 2 tomatoes, sliced
- 2 cups baby spinach
- 1 red onion, sliced
- Sea salt and ground black pepper, to taste
- 1 teaspoon lemon juice
- 1 teaspoon lemon zest
- 1 tablespoon olive oil
- 4 tablespoons tahini

COOKING STEPS

1. Put the couscous in a bowl; pour the boiling water to cover by about 1 inch. Cover and set aside for 5 to 8 minutes; fluff with a fork.

2. Place the couscous in a lightly greased cake pan. Transfer the pan to the air fryer basket and cook at 360° f about 20 minutes. Make sure to stir every 5 minutes to ensure even cooking.

3. Transfer the prepared couscous to a mixing bowl. Add the remaining ingredients; gently stir to combine. Bon appétit!

Nutrition: Calories 352 Fat 12g Carb 49g 16g Protein 26g

SPICY CAULIFLOWER RICE

10 minutes | **22 minutes** | **Brunch** | **02 Servings**

INGREDIENTS

- 1 cauliflower head, cut into florets
- 1/2 tsp cumin
- 1/2 tsp chili powder
- 6 onion spring, chopped
- 2 jalapenos, chopped
- 4 tbsp olive oil
- 1 zucchini, trimmed and cut into cubes
- 1/2 tsp paprika
- 1/2 tsp garlic powder
- 1/2 tsp cayenne pepper
- 1/2 tsp pepper
- 1/2 tsp salt

COOKING STEPS

1. Preheat the air fryer to 370° f.
2. Prepare food processor and put the cauliflower florets. Process until it looks like rice.
3. Transfer cauliflower rice into the air fryer baking pan and drizzle with half oil.
4. Place pan in the air fryer and cook for 12 minutes, stir halfway through.
5. Heat remaining oil in a small pan over medium heat.
6. Add zucchini and cook for 58 minutes.
7. Add onion and jalapenos and cook for 5 minutes.
8. Add spices and stir well. Set aside.
9. Add cauliflower rice to the zucchini mixture and stir well.
10. Serve and enjoy.

Nutrition: Calories 254; Fat 28 g; Carbs 13g; Sugar 5g; Protein 3g

RADISH HASH BROWNS

10 minutes | **13 minutes** | **Brunch** | **04 Servings**

INGREDIENTS

- 1 lb. Radishes, washed and cut off roots
- 1 tbsp olive oil
- 1/2 tsp paprika
- 1/2 tsp onion powder
- 1/2 tsp garlic powder
- 1 medium onion
- 1/4 tsp pepper
- 3/4 tsp sea salt

COOKING STEPS

1. Slice onion and radishes using a mandolin slicer.
2. Add sliced onion and radishes in a large mixing bowl and tossed with olive oil.
3. Transfer onion and radish slices to air fryer basket and cook at 360° f for 8 minutes. Shake basket twice.
4. Return onion and radish slices in a mixing bowl and toss with seasonings.
5. Again, cook onion, and radish slices in air fryer basket for 5 minutes at 400° f. Shake basket halfway through.
6. Serve and enjoy.

Nutrition: Calories 62; Fat 7g Carbohydrates 1 g Sugar 5 g Protein 2 g

Lunch

AIR FRIED BRUSSELS SPROUTS

05 minutes | 10 minutes | Lunch | 01 Servings

INGREDIENTS

- 1pound brussels sprouts
- 1 tablespoon coconut oil, melted
- 1 tablespoon unsalted vegan butter, melted

COOKING STEPS

1. Preheat the air fryer oven to 400°F (204C).

2. Prepare the Brussels sprouts by halving them, discarding any loose leaves.

3. Combine with the melted coconut oil and transfer to the air fryer basket. Set and cook for 10 minutes. Shake the basket once cooking. The sprouts are ready when they are partially caramelized.

4. Remove from the oven and serve with a topping of melted butter.

Nutrition: Calories: 45g Fat: 10g Carbs: 9g Protein: 4g

Lunch and Dinner

EASY ROSEMARY GREEN BEANS

05 minutes | 05 minutes | Lunch | 01 Servings

INGREDIENTS

- 1 tablespoon vegan butter, melted
- 2 tablespoons rosemary
- 1/2 teaspoon salt
- 3 cloves garlic, minced
- 3/4 cup chopped green beans

COOKING STEPS

1. Preheat the air fryer oven to 390°F (199C).
2. Combine the melted butter with the rosemary, salt, and minced garlic.
3. Toss in the green beans, coating them well. Transfer to the air fryer basket. Set air fryer time to 5 minutes.
4. Serve immediately.

Nutrition: Calories: 32 Fat: 3g Carbs: 8g Protein: 2g

GARLIC EGGPLANT SLICES

05 minutes | 15 minutes | Lunch | 01 Servings

INGREDIENTS

- 1 large eggplant, sliced
- 2 tablespoons olive oil
- ¼ teaspoon salt
- ½ teaspoon garlic powder

COOKING STEPS

1. Preheat the air fryer oven to 390°F (199C).
2. Put eggplant slices with the olive oil, salt, and garlic powder in a mixing bowl until evenly coated.
3. Put the slices in the air fryer basket. Place the baking pan and cook for 15 minutes.
4. Serve immediately.

Nutrition: Calories: 66 Fat: 7g Carbs: 1g Protein 2g

LEMONY FALAFEL

10 minutes | 15 minutes | Lunch | 08 Servings

INGREDIENTS

- 1 teaspoon cumin seeds
- ½ teaspoon coriander seeds
- 2 cups chickpeas, drained and rinsed
- ½ teaspoon red pepper flakes
- 3 cloves garlic
- ¼ cup chopped parsley
- ¼ cup chopped coriander
- ½ onion, diced
- 1 tablespoon juice from freshly squeezed lemon
- 3 tablespoons flour
- ½ teaspoon salt
- Cooking spray

COOKING STEPS

1. Cook the cumin and coriander seeds over medium heat.
2. Grind using a mortar and pestle.
3. Put all ingredients, except for the cooking spray, in a food processor and blend until a fine consistency is achieved.
4. Use the hands to mold the mixture into falafels and spritz with the cooking spray.
5. Preheat the air fryer oven to 400° F (204C).
6. Transfer the falafels to the air fryer basket in a single layer. Cook until golden brown. Serve warm.

Nutrition: Calories: 56 Fat: 1g Carbs: 9g Protein: 3g

SWEET AND SOUR TOFU

15 minutes | 20 minutes | Lunch | 02 Servings

INGREDIENTS

- 2 teaspoons apple cider vinegar
- 1 tablespoon sugar
- 1 tablespoon soy sauce
- 3 teaspoons lime juice
- 1 teaspoon ground ginger
- 1 teaspoon garlic powder
- ½ block firm tofu pressed to remove excess liquid and cut into cubes
- 1 teaspoon cornstarch
- 2 green onions, chopped
- Toasted sesame seeds, for garnish

COOKING STEPS

1. In a bowl, thoroughly combine the apple cider vinegar, sugar, soy sauce, lime juice, ground ginger, and garlic powder.
2. Cover the tofu with this mixture and leave to marinate for at least 30 minutes.
3. Preheat the air fryer oven to 400°F (204C).
4. Transfer the tofu to the air fryer basket, keeping any excess marinade for the sauce.
5. Cook the tofu for 20 minutes, or until crispy.
6. In the meantime, thicken the sauce with the cornstarch over medium low heat.
7. Serve the cooked tofu with the sauce, green onions, and sesame seeds.

Nutrition: Calories: 207 Fat: 11g Carbs: 13g Protein: 18g

CRISPY CHICKPEAS

05 minutes | 15 minutes | Lunch | 04 Servings

INGREDIENTS

- 1 can (15ounces / 425g) chickpeas, drained but not rinsed
- 2 tablespoons olive oil
- 1 teaspoon salt
- 2 tablespoons lemon juice

COOKING STEPS

1. Preheat the air fryer oven to 400ºF (204ºC).
2. Put and mix all ingredients in a bowl. Transfer this mixture to the air fryer basket.
3. Put mixture into baking pan and slide into rack position 2, select air fry, and set time to 15 minutes, ensuring the chickpeas become nice and crispy.
4. Serve immediately.

Nutrition: Calories: 132 Fat: 6g Carbs: 14g Protein: 5g

SKINNY PUMPKIN CHIPS

10 minutes | **13 minutes** | **Lunch** | **02 Servings**

INGREDIENTS

- 1 pound pumpkin, cut into sticks
- 1 tablespoon coconut oil
- 1/2 teaspoon rosemary
- 1/2 teaspoon basil
- Salt and ground black pepper, to taste

COOKING STEPS

1. Start by preheating the air fryer to 395 ° F. Brush the pumpkin sticks with coconut oil.
2. Put the spices and combine well.
3. Cook for 13 minutes, shaking the basket halfway through the cooking time.
4. Serve with mayonnaise. Bon appétit!

Nutrition: Calories 118 Fat 7g Carbs 17g Protein 2g

RAINBOW VEGETABLE FRITTERS

10 minutes | 12 minutes | Lunch | 02 Servings

INGREDIENTS

- 1 zucchini, grated and squeezed
- 1 cup corn kernels
- 1/2 cup canned green peas
- 4 tablespoons all-purpose flour
- 2 tablespoons fresh shallots, minced
- 1 teaspoon fresh garlic, minced
- 1 tablespoon peanut oil
- Sea salt
- Ground black pepper, to taste
- 1 teaspoon cayenne pepper

COOKING STEPS

5. Combine well all ingredients in a mixing bowl until everything is incorporated.
6. Shape the mixture into patties. Put cooking spray in the air fryer basket.
7. Cook in the preheated air fryer at 365 °F for 6 minutes. Turn and cook the other side for additional 6 minutes.
8. Serve immediately and enjoy!

Nutrition: Calories: 215 Fat: 32g Carbs: 6g Protein: 4g

MEDITERRANEAN VEGETABLE SKEWERS

15 minutes | 13 minutes | Lunch | 04 Servings

INGREDIENTS

- 2 medium-sized zucchinis
- 2 red bell peppers
- 1 green bell pepper
- 1 red onion, cut into 1inch pieces
- 2 tablespoons olive oil
- Sea salt, to taste
- 1/2 teaspoon black pepper, preferably freshly cracked
- 1/2 teaspoon red pepper flakes

COOKING STEPS

1. Cut the zucchinis, red and green bell peppers into 1inch pieces
2. Rinse the wooden skewers in water for 15 minutes.
3. Thread the vegetables on skewers; drizzle olive oil all over the vegetable skewers; sprinkle with spices.
4. Preheat at 400° F and cook for 13 minutes. Serve warm and enjoy!

Nutrition: Calories 138 Fat 12g Carbs 12g Protein 2g

FRIED PEPPERS WITH SRIRACHA MAYO

10 minutes | 14 minutes | Lunch | 02 Servings

INGREDIENTS

- 4 bell peppers, seeded and sliced (1inch pieces)
- 1 onion, sliced (1inch pieces)
- 1 tablespoon olive oil
- 1/2 teaspoon dried rosemary
- 1/2 teaspoon dried basil
- Kosher salt, to taste
- 1/4 teaspoon ground black pepper
- 1/3 cup mayonnaise
- 1/3 teaspoon sriracha

COOKING STEPS

1. Mix the onions and bell peppers with the olive oil, rosemary, basil, salt, and black pepper.
2. Place the peppers and onions on an even layer in the cooking basket.
3. Cook at 400° F for 12 to 14 minutes.
4. Meanwhile, make the sauce by whisking the mayonnaise and sriracha. Serve immediately.

Nutrition: Calories: 15 Fiber: 5g Carbs: 5g Protein: 5g

BALSAMIC ROOT VEGETABLES

10 minutes | 15 minutes | Lunch | 01 Servings

INGREDIENTS

- 2 potatoes, cut into 1 1/2inch piece
- 2 carrots, cut into 1 1/2inch piece
- 2 parsnips, cut into 1 1/2inch piece
- 1 onion, cut into 1 1/2inch piece
- Pink Himalayan salt and ground black pepper, to taste
- 1/4 teaspoon smoked paprika
- 1 teaspoon garlic powder
- 1/2 teaspoon dried thyme
- 1/2 teaspoon dried marjoram
- 2 tablespoons olive oil
- 2 tablespoons balsamic vinegar

COOKING STEPS

1. Toss all ingredients in a large mixing dish.
2. Roast in the preheated air fryer at 400 ° F for 10 minutes. Shake the basket and cook for 7 minutes more.
3. Serve with some extra fresh herbs if desired. Bon appétit!

Nutrition: Calories: 164 Fat: 4g Carbs: 32g Protein: 3g

TOFU NUGGETS WITH GINGER SOY MARINADE

10 minutes | 25 minutes | Lunch | 04 Servings

INGREDIENTS

- Extra firm tofu (14 oz)
- Arrowroot flour (0.25 c.)
- Garlic powder (1 tsp)
- Smoked paprika (0.5 tsp)
- Ground cumin (0.5 tsp)
- Salt (1 tsp)
- Soy Sauce (3 Tbsp.)
- Coconut sugar (2 Tbsp.)
- Agave nectar (2 Tbsp.)
- Ginger (1 Tbsp., freshly grated)
- Garlic powder (1 tsp)
- White sesame seeds (1 tsp)
- Scallion (1, chopped)
- Avocado oil

COOKING STEPS

1. Slice tofu to preferred bite sized squares. Remove excess moisture by pressing with a towel or paper towel.

2. Place tofu squares in a bowl. Mix in the arrowroot flour, smoked paprika, salt, cumin, and garlic powder. Coat tofu evenly.

3. Spray avocado oil in fryer and place cubes in a single layer. Spray tops of tofu squares with oil as well—Cook at 350 °F for 10 minutes.

4. Toss tofu and settle back to one layer to cook for another 15 minutes.

5. In a large bowl, whisk soy sauce, coconut sugar, avocado oil, ginger, agave nectar, pepper, sesame seeds, and garlic powder.

6. Place fried tofu into the bowl with the sauce and toss to coat evenly.

7. Once plated, pour remaining sauce on meal and garnish with sesame seeds and scallion.

Nutrition: Calories: 139 Carb: 18g Fat: 4g Protein: 10g

THAI VEGGIE BITES

10 minutes | 25 minutes | Lunch | 04 Servings

INGREDIENTS

- Broccoli crown (1)
- Cauliflower (1 0.5, half a crown used as cauliflower rice)
- Large carrots (6)
- Garden peas (1 c.)
- Large onion (1)
- Zucchini (1)
- Leeks (2, washed and sliced thin)
- Coconut milk (1 can)
- Flour (50g)
- Ginger (1cm cube, peeled then grated)
- Garlic puree (1 Tbsp.)
- Olive oil (1 Tbsp.)
- Thai green curry paste (1 Tbsp.)
- Coriander (1 Tbsp.)
- Mixed spice (1 Tbsp.)
- Cumin (1 tsp)
- Salt (to taste)
- Pepper (to taste)

COOKING STEPS

1. In a skillet, pan fry onion, ginger, and garlic until brown.
2. Place vegetables save from the zucchini and leek, in a steamer until they are almost cooked through.
3. Add the leek, zucchini, and curry paste to the skillet and cook for 5 minutes on medium heat.
4. Add coconut milk and the seasoning mix. Mix in the cauliflower rice. Simmer for 10 minutes.
5. Add in the steamed veggies and stir. Stick in the fridge and allow the mixture to cool.
6. Once cooled, form bite sized lumps and place in the fryer—Cook for 10 minutes at 350 °F.

Nutrition: Calories: 117 Carb: 12g Fat: 7g Protein: 4g

Lunch and Dinner

COCONUT FRENCH TOAST

05 minutes | 04 minutes | Lunch | 01 Servings

INGREDIENTS

- Gluten free bread (2 slices)
- Lite culinary coconut milk (0.5 c.)
- Baking powder (1 tsp)
- Unsweetened shredded coconut (0.5 c.)

COOKING STEPS

1. In a bowl, mix the coconut milk and baking powder.
2. Take the shredded coconut and spread it on a plate.
3. Take both slices of bread and soak in the coconut milk, then coat with shredded coconut.
4. Place the slices of bread in the fryer—fry for 4 minutes at 350° F.

Nutrition: Calories: 627 Carb: 56g Fat: 42g Protein: 33g

BEIGNETS

15 minutes | **02 hours** | **Lunch** | **24 Servings**

INGREDIENTS

- Powdered sugar (1 c.)
- Full fat coconut milk (1 c.)
- Baking yeast (1 0.5 tsp)
- Coconut oil (2 Tbsp.)
- Aquafaba (2 Tbsp.)
- Vanilla extract (2 tsp)
- Unbleached white flour (3 c.)

COOKING STEPS

1. Warm the coconut milk just enough to be tolerable with your finger. Pour in a bowl or stand mixer with the yeast. Let stand for 10 minutes.

2. Mix in warmed coconut oil (to avoid clumping) vanilla extract, and aquafaba. Add only a cup. of flour at a time. The paddle attachment is recommended.

3. Switch to a dough hook when the dough no longer sticks to the sides and knead for 3 minutes.

4. Remove the dough and let sit, covered, in a bowl for 1 hour to allow it to rise.

5. Sprinkle flour on a cutting board and form dough into a rectangle about a third of an inch thick. Cut into 24 squares and proof for 30 more minutes.

6. Set air fryer to 390 °F and place 1 layer of beignets at a time. Cook for one side, then flip and continue cooking for 2 minutes or until golden brown.

7. Remove beignets and coat them with powdered sugar.

Nutrition: Calories: 106 Carb: 17g Fat: 3g Protein: 6g

Lunch and Dinner

POTATO WEDGES IN CASHEW SAUCE

10 minutes | 35 minutes | Lunch | 04 Servings

INGREDIENTS

- Fingerling potatoes (1 lb.)
- Olive oil (1 tsp)
- Salt (1 tsp)
- Ground black pepper (1 tsp)
- Garlic powder (0.5 tsp)
- Raw cashews (0.5 c.)
- Turmeric (0.5 tsp)
- Paprika (0.5 tsp)
- Nutritional yeast (2 Tbsp.)
- Lemon juice (1 tsp

COOKING STEPS

1. Set fryer to 400 °F. Wash and cut the potatoes into wedges. Mix in oil, pepper, salt, and garlic powder. Coat evenly.

2. Cook for 16 minutes, shake at the 8minute mark.

3. To create the sauce, combine the cashews, yeast, paprika, turmeric, and lemon juice in a blender. Add water as needed, no more than 25 c. Should be necessary.

4. Place the potato wedges into a compatible pan or parchment paper. Drizzle the sauce of the wedges and stick back into the fryer to cook for 2 minutes.

Nutrition: Calories 182 Carb 21g Fat 9g Protein 7g

FRUIT CRUMBLE

10 minutes | 30 minutes | Lunch | 02 Servings

INGREDIENTS

- Apple (1, diced finely)
- Frozen fruit of choice (0.5 c., we'll go with strawberries)
- Brown rice flour (0.25 c.)
- Sugar (2 Tbsp.)
- Cinnamon (0.5 tsp, ground)
- vegan butter (2 Tbsp.)

COOKING STEPS

1. Set fryer to 350 °F. Pour the apple bits and frozen strawberries in a compatible pan.
2. Get another bowl and mix well all other ingredients.
3. Pour over the fruit and fry for 15 minutes.

Nutrition: Calories: 210 Carb: 50g Fat: 19g Protein: 4g

CAJUN FRENCH FRY SANDWICH WITH MUSHROOM GRAVY

10 minutes | 35 minutes | Lunch | 04 Servings

INGREDIENTS

- Russet potatoes (4, cut into wedges or fries)
- Olive oil (1 Tbsp. & 2 tsp)
- Cajun seasoning (1 tsp)
- Smoked paprika (0.5 tsp)
- Salt (pinch)
- Granulated garlic (pinch)
- Black pepper (pinch, ground)
- Mushrooms (3 c., chopped)
- Soy sauce (2 tsp)
- Vegan Worcestershire sauce (2 tsp)
- Tapioca starch (1 Tbsp.)
- Bread of choice
- Sandwich condiments of choice (lettuce, tomatoes, etc.)

COOKING STEPS

1. Pour boiling water onto the fries and let soak for roughly 15 minutes. Strain.
2. Mix fries with oil, seasoning, salt, garlic, paprika, and black pepper.
3. Take fries and cook in air fryer basket for 5 minutes at 350 degrees. Shake and then cook another 5 minutes.
4. Increase heat to 400 °F and cook for 5 minutes. Shake and cook another 5.
5. During downtime, add 1 Tbsp. of oil to a skillet. On medium heat, add mushrooms and sauté until dehydrated. Add Worcestershire & soy sauces and cook for approximately 2 minutes.
6. Add roughly half a cup of water and whisk tapioca starch into the mix. Cook until thick, raising temperature as necessary.
7. Take fries, and gravy, and assemble sandwich as you wish.

Nutrition: Calories: 555 Carb: 104g Fat: 10g Protein: 20g

VEGAN FRENCH TOAST

05 minutes | **10 minutes** | **Lunch** | **04 Servings**

INGREDIENTS

- Rolled oats (1 c.)
- Pecans (1 c.)
- Ground flax seed (2 Tbsp.)
- Ground cinnamon (1 tsp)
- Whole grain vegan bread (8 pieces)
- Nondairy milk (0.75 c.)
- Maple Syrup

COOKING STEPS

1. Throw oats, nuts, flaxseed, and cinnamon into a blender or food processor and process into a coarse grind. Pour mixture into a pan.

2. Pour the nondairy milk into a separate container and soak bread slices for approximately 15 seconds on each side.

3. Coat both slides of bread slices with the previously ground mixture and fit into the fryer basket. Do not overlap. Cook for 3 minutes at 350 °F, then flip and cook another 3 minutes.

4. Top with maple syrup.

Nutrition: Calories: 183 Carb: 32g Fat: 4g Protein: 6g

Dinner

Lunch and Dinner

FLAVORSOME BITTER GOURD

25 minutes   20 minutes   Dinner   04 Servings

INGREDIENTS

- 4 tablespoons of oil
- ½ teaspoon of pepper
- ½ teaspoon of salt
- ½ teaspoon of turmeric
- 8 oz of vegan bitter gourd
- 4 onions
- ½ teaspoon of red chili pepper
- ½ teaspoon of onion powder
- ½ teaspoon of paprika
- 1/3 teaspoon of cumin
- 3 cloves of garlic

COOKING STEPS

1. Wash and clean the vegan bitter gourd.
2. Cut it in the pieces.
3. Then rub them with pepper, salt, turmeric, red chili pepper, onion powder, paprika, cumin and chopped garlic.
4. Cut onions in the rings.
5. Blend everything well.
6. Sprinkle the air fryer with oil.
7. Preheat it to 350F.
8. Cook the meal for 10 minutes.
9. Then shake everything and cook for 10 minutes more.
10. 1 serve hot with parsley.

Nutrition: Calories: 95 Fat: 2,1g Carb: 6,2g Protein: 1,1g

Lunch and Dinner

SPINACH WITH GROUNDNUTS

10 minutes | 15 minutes | Dinner | 04 Servings

INGREDIENTS

- 1 tablespoon of vegetable oil
- ½ tablespoon of red chili pepper
- ¼ tablespoon of cumin
- ½ teaspoon of salt
- ½ teaspoon of pepper
- 2 tomatoes
- 3 oz of groundnuts
- 6 oz of spinach
- 3 cloves of garlic
- ½ teaspoon of paprika
- ½ teaspoon of onion powder

COOKING STEPS

1. Wash and chop spinach in the pieces.
2. Then add red chili pepper, oil, cumin, salt, pepper, groundnuts, garlic, paprika and onion powder.
3. Blend everything well.
4. After that chop tomatoes in the pieces.
5. Blend everything well.
6. Sprinkle the air fryer with oil.
7. Preheat it to 350°F for 3 minutes.
8. Cook the meal in the air fryer for 10 minutes.
9. Then shake well and cook for 5 minutes more.
10. 1serve hot with parsley and basil leaves.

Nutrition: Calories: 103 Fat: 2,1g Carb: 3,8g Protein: 1,1g

FLAVORSOME AND FIERY AUBERGINE

15 minutes | 20 minutes | Dinner | 04 Servings

INGREDIENTS

- 9 oz of aubergine
- 2 onions
- 5 cloves of garlic
- ½ teaspoon of salt
- ½ teaspoon of pepper
- 2 tablespoons of oil
- 1 tablespoon of sesame seeds
- 1 tablespoon of coriander seeds
- 1 tablespoon of cumin
- 4 tablespoons of vegan butter
- ½ teaspoon of onion powder
- ½ teaspoon of dry herbs
- ½ teaspoon of parsley

COOKING STEPS

1. Wash and clean aubergine.
2. Then cut them in the pieces.
3. Rub vegetables with salt, pepper, garlic, sesame seeds, cumin, coriander seeds, butter, parsley, onion powder and dry herbs.
4. Chop onions in the rings.
5. Blend everything.
6. Sprinkle the air fryer with oil.
7. Preheat it for 5 minutes to 300°F.
8. Then cook the meal for 10 minutes.
9. Blend everything well and cook for 5 minutes.
10. 1serve hot with sauce.

Nutrition: Calories: 112 Fat: 3,2g Carb: 7g Protein: 1,2g

TOFU WITH PEANUT DIPPING SAUCE

05 minutes | 08 minutes | Dinner | 06 Servings

INGREDIENTS

- 16 oz. Cubed firm tofu
- 185g all-purpose flour
- ½ teaspoon Himalayan salt
- ½ teaspoon ground black pepper
- Olive oil spray
- For the dipping sauce:
- 1/3 c. Smooth low-sodium peanut butter
- 1 teaspoon minced garlic
- 2 tbsps. Light soy sauce
- 1 tablespoon fresh lime juice
- 1 teaspoon brown sugar
- 1/3 c. Water
- 2 tbsps. Chopped roasted

COOKING STEPS

1. In a bowl, mix all dipping sauce ingredients. Cover it with plastic wrap and keep refrigerated until ready to serve.
2. To make the fried tofu, season all-purpose flour with salt and pepper.
3. Coat the tofu cubes with the flour mixture. Spray with oil.
4. Preheat your air fryer to 390°F.
5. Place coated tofu in the cooking basket. Careful not to overcrowd them.
6. Cook until browned for approximately 8 minutes.
7. Serve with prepared peanut dipping sauce.
8. Enjoy!

Nutrition: Calories 256 Fat 11g Carb 22g Protein 14 g.

BROWN RICE, SPINACH AND TOFU FRITTATA

05 minutes | 55 minutes | Dinner | 04 Servings

INGREDIENTS

- ½ cup baby spinach, chopped
- ½ cup kale, chopped
- ½ onion, chopped
- ½ teaspoon turmeric
- 1 ¾ cups brown rice, cooked
- 1 flax egg (1 tablespoon flaxseed meal + 3 tablespoon cold water1 package firm tofu
- 1 tablespoon olive oil
- 1 yellow pepper, chopped
- 2 tablespoons soy sauce
- 2 teaspoons arrowroot powder
- 2 teaspoons Dijon mustard
- 2/3 cup almond milk
- 3 big mushrooms, chopped
- 3 tablespoons nutritional yeast
- 4 cloves garlic, crushed
- 4 spring onions, chopped
- A handful of basil leaves, chopped

COOKING STEPS

1. Preheat the air fryer oven to 375°F. Grease pan that will fit inside the air fryer oven.

2. Prepare the frittata crust by mixing the brown rice and flax egg. Press the rice onto the baking dish until you form a crust. Brush with a little oil and cook for 10 minutes.

3. Meanwhile, heat olive oil in a skillet over medium flame and sauté the garlic and onions for 2 minutes.

4. Add the pepper and mushroom and continue stirring for 3 minutes.

5. Stir in the kale, spinach, spring onions, and basil. Remove from the pan and set aside.

6. In a food processor, pulse together the tofu, mustard, turmeric, soy sauce, nutritional yeast, vegan milk and arrowroot powder. Pour in a mixing bowl and stir in the sautéed vegetables.

7. Pour the vegan frittata mixture over the rice crust and cook in the air fryer oven for 40 minutes.

Nutrition: Calories 226 Fat 05g Carb 16 Protein 16g

COCONUT CURRY VEGETABLE RICE BOWLS

10 minutes | 35 minutes | Dinner | 04 Servings

INGREDIENTS

- 2/3 cup uncooked brown rice
- 1 tsp. Curry powder
- 3/4 tsp. Salt divided
- 1 cup chopped green onion
- 1 cup sliced red bell pepper
- 1 tbsp. Grated ginger
- 1 1/2 tbsp. Sugar
- 1 cup matchstick carrots
- 1 cup chopped red cabbage
- 8 oz. Sliced water chestnuts
- 15 oz. No salt added chickpeas
- 13 oz. Coconut milk

COOKING STEPS

1. Add rice, water, curry powder, and 1/4 tsp. Of the salt in the instant pot. Pressure cook for 15 minutes. Sauté for 2 minutes and serve.

Nutrition: Calories 630 Fat 11g Carb 25g Protein 25g

TOFU WITH STICKY ORANGE SAUCE

15 minutes | 20 minutes | Dinner | 00 Servings

INGREDIENTS

- 1-pound extra-firm tofu drained and pressed (or use super firm tofu)
- 1 teaspoon tamari
- 1 teaspoon cornstarch, (or arrowroot powder)

For sauce:
- 1 teaspoon orange zest
- 1/3 cup oranges juice
- 1/2 cup water
- 2 tablespoons cornstarch (or arrowroot powder)
- 1/4 teaspoon ground pepper flakes
- 1 teaspoon fresh ginger, minced
- 1 tablespoon garlic, minced
- 1 teaspoon pure maple syrup

COOKING STEPS

1. Cut tofu into dices.
2. Put tofu in a Ziploc bag. Add tamarind and seal the bag. Stir the bag until all the tofu is covered with tamarind.
3. Add a tablespoon of cornstarch to the bag. Stir again until the tofu is coated. Set the tofu aside for at least 15 minutes to marinate.
4. Meanwhile, add all the sauce elements to a small bowl and mix with a spoon.
5. Place the tofu in an air fryer. You in all probability want to do this in two batches.
6. Cook the tofu in 390°F steps for 10 minutes, adding it for 10 minutes.
7. After you finish cooking the batches of tofu, add it all to a pan on medium-high heat. Give the sauce a stir and pour over the tofu.
8. Mix tofu and sauce until it thickens, and the tofu becomes hot.
9. Serve directly with rice and boiled vegetables if desired.

Nutrition: Calories 190 Fat 3g Carb 16g Protein 10g

Side Dish Recipes

BATTER-FRIED SCALLIONS

05 minutes | **05 minutes** | **Side Dish** | **04 Servings**

INGREDIENTS

- Trimmed scallion bunches,
- White wine, 1 cup
- Salt, 1 tsp.
- Flour, 1 cup
- Black pepper, 1 tsp.

COOKING STEPS

1. Set the air fryer to heat up to 390°f. Using a bowl, add and mix the white wine, flour and stir until it gets smooth. Add the salt, the black pepper and mix again. Dip each scallion into the flour mixture until it is properly covered and remove any excess batter. Grease your air fryer basket with nonstick cooking spray and add the scallions. At this point, you may need to work in batches.

2. Leave the scallions to cook for 5 minutes or until it has a golden-brown color and crispy texture, while still shaking it after every 2 minutes. Carefully remove it from your air fryer and check if it's properly done. Then allow it to cool before serving. Serve and enjoy.

Nutrition: Calories 190 Fat 22g Carb 9g Protein 4g

BEETS AND CARROTS

10 minutes | **12 minutes** | **Side Dish** | **04 Servings**

INGREDIENTS

- 4 carrots whole
- 4 sliced young beetroots
- ¼ tsp. Black pepper
- 1 tsp. Olive oil
- ¼ tsp. Salt
- 1 tbsps. Lemon juice

COOKING STEPS

1. Preheat air fryer to a temperature of 400°F (200°C)
2. Transfer beetroots and carrots to air fryer basket and sprinkle salt and pepper. Drizzle olive oil and toss to combine.
3. Leave to cook for 12 minutes. Shake the basket of fryer after halftime. Remove from the air fryer and drizzle lemon juice. Serve and enjoy!

Nutrition: Calories 51 Fat 3 Carb 8 g Protein 2 g

Side Dish Recipes

BROCCOLI CRISPS

10 minutes | 12 minutes | Side Dish | 04 Servings

INGREDIENTS

- Large chopped broccoli head,
- Salt, 1 tsp.
- Olive oil, 2 tbsps.
- Black pepper, 1 tsp.

COOKING STEPS

1. Set the air fryer to heat up to 360°F.
2. Using a bowl, add and toss the broccoli florets with olive oil, salt, and black pepper.
3. Add the broccoli florets and cook it for 12 minutes, then shake after 6 minutes.
4. Carefully remove it from your air fryer and allow it to cool off.
5. Serve and enjoy!

Nutrition: Calories 20 Fat 1.2g Carb 3g Protein 2g

MAYO BRUSSELS SPROUTS

05 minutes | 15 minutes | Side Dish | 04 Servings

INGREDIENTS

- 1-pound brussels sprouts, trimmed and halved
- Salt and black pepper to taste
- 6 teaspoons olive oil
- ½ cup mayonnaise
- 2 tablespoons garlic, minced

COOKING STEPS

1. In your air fryer, mix the sprouts, salt, pepper, and oil; toss well.
2. Cook the sprouts at 390 °F for 15 minutes.
3. Transfer them to a bowl; then add the mayonnaise and the garlic and toss.
4. Divide between plates and serve as a side dish.

Nutrition: Calories 190 Fat 8 Carb 9 Protein 4

GREEN BEANS AND SHALLOTS

- 05 minutes
- 25 minutes
- Side Dish
- 04 Servings

INGREDIENTS

- 1½ pounds green beans, trimmed
- Salt and black pepper to taste
- ½ pound shallots, chopped
- ¼ cup walnuts, chopped
- 2 tablespoons olive oil

COOKING STEPS

1. In your air fryer, mix all ingredients and toss.
2. Cook at 350 °F for 25 minutes.
3. Divide between plates and serve as a side dish.

Nutrition: Calories 182 Fat 3 Carb 11 Protein 7

HERBED ROASTED POTATOES

05 minutes | **17 minutes** | **Side Dish** | **04 Servings**

INGREDIENTS

- 1 teaspoon crushed dried thyme
- 1 teaspoon ground black pepper
- 2 tablespoons olive oil
- 1/2 tablespoon crushed dried rosemary
- 3 potatoes, peeled, washed and cut into wedges
- 1/2 teaspoon seasoned salt

COOKING STEPS

1. Lay the potatoes in the air fryer cooking basket; drizzle olive oil over your potatoes.
2. Then, cook for 17 minutes at 353 °F.
3. Toss with the seasonings and serve warm with your favorite salad on the side.

Nutrition: Calories 163 Fat 7 Carb 38g Protein 3g

EASY FRIZZLED LEEKS

25 minutes | **18 minutes** | **Side Dish** | **06 Servings**

INGREDIENTS

- 1/2 teaspoon porcini powder
- 1 1/2 cup rice flour
- 1 tablespoon vegetable oil
- 3 medium-sized leeks, slice into julienne strips
- 2 large-sized dishes with ice water
- 2 teaspoons onion powder
- Fine sea salt and cayenne pepper, to taste

COOKING STEPS

1. Allow the leeks to soak in ice water for about 25 minutes; drain well.

2. Place the rice flour, salt, cayenne pepper, onions powder, and porcini powder into a resealable bag. Add the celery and shake to coat well.

3. Drizzle vegetable oil over the seasoned leeks. Air fry at 390 °F for about 18 minutes; turn them halfway through the cooking time. Serve with homemade mayonnaise or any other sauce for dipping. Enjoy!

Nutrition: Calories 291 Fat 6g Carb 53g Protein 7g

Fruit and Vegetables

Fruit & Vegetables

TOASTY PEPPER BITES

06 minutes | 15-30 minutes | Fruit & Vegetables | 06 Servings

INGREDIENTS

- 1 medium-sized red bell pepper cut into small pieces
- 1 medium-sized yellow bell pepper cut up into small pieces
- 1 medium-sized green bell pepper cut up into small pieces
- 3 tablespoons of balsamic vinegar
- 2 tablespoon of olive oil
- 1 tablespoon of minced garlic
- 1/2 teaspoon of dried basil
- 1/2 a teaspoon of dried parsley
- Kosher salt as needed
- Pepper as needed

COOKING STEPS

1. Take a mixing bowl and add all of the diced-up bell peppers
2. Mix them well and add olive oil, garlic, balsamic vinegar, basil and parsley
3. Mix them well
4. Season with salt and pepper
5. Stir well
6. Cover and allow it to chill for 30 minutes
7. Preheat your fryer to 390 °f
8. Transfer the peppers to your frying basket and cook for 10-15 minutes
9. Serve and enjoy!

Nutrition: Calories 98 Carb 17g Fat 7g Protein 5g

PLATTER OF BRUSSELS AND PINE NUTS

10 minutes | 36 minutes | Fruit & Vegetables | 06 Servings

INGREDIENTS

- 15 ounces of brussels sprouts
- 1 tablespoon of olive oil
- 1 and a 3/4 ounce of drained raisins
- Juice of 1 orange
- 1 and a 3/4-ounce toasted pine nuts

COOKING STEPS

1. Take a pot of boiling water and add sprouts, boil for 4 minutes
2. Transfer them to cold water and drain them, store them in a freezer and allow them to cool
3. Take raising and soak them in orange juice for 20 minutes
4. Preheat your fryer to 392 degrees Fahrenheit
5. Take a pan and pour oil and stir fry your sprouts
6. Transfer the sprouts to the cooking basket and roast for 15 minutes
7. Serve the sprouts with a garnish of raisins, pine nuts, orange juice
8. Enjoy!

Nutrition: Calories 267 Fat 15g Carb 12 Protein 6g

CRISPY ROASTED BROCCOLI

45 minutes | **10 minutes** | **Fruit & Vegetables** | **02 Servings**

INGREDIENTS

- ¼ tsp. Masala
- ½ tsp. Red chili powder
- ½ tsp. Salt
- ¼ tsp. Turmeric powder
- 1 tbsp. Chickpea flour
- 2 tbsp. vegan Yogurt
- 1 pound broccoli

COOKING STEPS

1. Cut broccoli up into florets. Soak in bowl of water with 2 teaspoons of salt for at least half an hour to remove impurities.
2. Take out broccoli florets from water and let drain. Wipe down thoroughly.
3. Mix all other ingredients together to create a marinade.
4. Toss broccoli florets in the marinade. Cover and chill 15-30 minutes.
5. Preheat air fryer to 390°f. Place marinated broccoli florets into the fryer. Cook 10 minutes.
6. 5 minutes into cooking shake the basket. Florets will be crispy when done.

Nutrition: Calories 96 Fat 3g Carb 23 protein 7g

CINNAMON BUTTERNUT SQUASH FRIES

10 minutes | 10 minutes | Fruit & Vegetables | 02 Servings

INGREDIENTS

- 1 pinch of salt
- 1 tbsp. Powdered unprocessed sugar
- ½ tsp. Nutmeg
- 2 tsp. Cinnamon
- 1 tbsp. Coconut oil

10 ounces precut butternut squash fries

COOKING STEPS

1. In a plastic bag, pour in all ingredients. Coat fries with other components till coated and sugar is dissolved.

2. Spread coated fries into a single layer in the air fryer. Cook 10 minutes at 390°f until crispy.

Nutrition: Calories 175 Fat 8g Carb 13 Protein 1g

CHEESY ARTICHOKES

10 minutes | 14 minutes | Fruit & Vegetables | 04 Servings

INGREDIENTS

- 4 artichokes, trimmed and halved
- 1 cup vegan cheddar cheese, shredded
- 2 tablespoons olive oil
- A pinch of salt and black pepper
- 3 garlic cloves, minced
- 1 teaspoon garlic powder

COOKING STEPS

1. In your air fryer's basket, combine the artichokes with the oil, cheese and the other ingredients, toss and cook at 400° f for 14 minutes.
2. Divide everything between plates and serve.

Nutrition: Calories 181 Fat 8 Carbs 12 Protein 8

PAPRIKA TOMATOES

10 minutes | 15 minutes | Fruit & Vegetables | 04 Servings

INGREDIENTS

- 1 pound cherry tomatoes, halved
- 1 tablespoon sweet paprika
- 2 tablespoons olive oil
- 2 garlic cloves, minced
- 1 tablespoon lime juice
- 1 tablespoon chives, chopped

COOKING STEPS

1. In your air fryer's basket, combine the tomatoes with the paprika and the other ingredients, toss and cook at a temperature of 370° f for 15 minutes.

2. Divide between plates and serve.

Nutrition: Calories 131 Fat 4 Carbs 10 Protein 3

AVOCADO AND TOMATO SALAD

10 minutes | 12 minutes | Fruit & Vegetables | 04 Servings

INGREDIENTS

- 1 pound tomatoes, cut into wedges
- 2 avocados, peeled, pitted and sliced
- 2 tablespoons avocado oil
- 1 red onion, sliced
- 1 tablespoon balsamic vinegar
- Salt and black pepper to the taste
- 1 tablespoon cilantro, chopped

COOKING STEPS

1. In your air fryer, combine the tomatoes with the avocados and the other ingredients, toss and cook at 360° f for 12 minutes.
2. Divide between plates and serve.

Nutrition: Calories 144 Fat 7 Carbs 8 Protein 6

SESAME BROCCOLI MIX

05 minutes | 14 minutes | Fruit & Vegetables | 04 Servings

INGREDIENTS

- 1 pound broccoli florets
- 1 tablespoon sesame oil
- 1 teaspoon sesame seeds, toasted
- 1 red onion, sliced
- 1 tablespoon lime juice
- 1 teaspoon chili powder
- Salt and black pepper to the taste

COOKING STEPS

1. In your air fryer, combine the broccoli with the oil, sesame seeds and the other ingredients, toss and cook at 380° f for 14 minutes.
2. Divide between plates and serve.

Nutrition: Calories 141 Fat 3 Fiber 4 Carbs 4 Protein 2

Fruit & Vegetables

CABBAGE SAUTÉ

| 05 minutes | 15 minutes | Fruit & Vegetables | 04 Servings |

INGREDIENTS

- 1 pound red cabbage, shredded
- 1 tablespoon balsamic vinegar
- 2 red onions, sliced
- 1 tablespoon olive oil
- 1 tablespoon dill, chopped

Salt and black pepper to the taste

COOKING STEPS

1. Heat up air fryer with oil at 380° f, add the cabbage, onions and the other ingredients, toss and cook for 15 minutes.
2. Divide between plates and serve.

Nutrition: Calories 100 Fat 4 Carbs 7 Protein 2

TOMATOES AND KIDNEY BEANS

10 minutes | 20 minutes | Fruit & Vegetables | 04 Servings

INGREDIENTS

- 1 pound cherry tomatoes, halved
- 1 cup canned kidney beans, drained
- 2 tablespoons balsamic vinegar
- 2 tablespoons olive oil
- 3 garlic cloves, minced
- Salt and black pepper to the taste
- 1 tablespoon chives, chopped

COOKING STEPS

1. In your air fryer, combine the cherry tomatoes with the beans and the other ingredients, toss and cook at 380° f for 20 minutes.
2. Divide between plates and serve.

Nutrition: Calories 101 Fat 3 Carbs 4 Protein 26

GLAZED MUSHROOMS

10 minutes | 15 minutes | Fruit & Vegetables | 04 Servings

INGREDIENTS

- ½ cup low sodium soy sauce
- 4 tablespoons fresh lemon juice
- 1 tablespoon maple syrup
- 4 garlic cloves, finely chopped
- Ground black pepper, as required
- 20 ounces fresh cremini mushrooms, halved

COOKING STEPS

1. Add the soy sauce, lemon juice, maple syrup, garlic and black pepper and mix well. Set aside.
2. Place the mushroom into the greased baking pan in a single layer.
3. Select "air fry" of digital air fryer oven and then adjust the temperature to 350° f.
4. Set the timer for 15 minutes and press "start/stop" to begin cooking.
5. When the unit beeps to show that it is preheated, insert the baking pan in the oven.
6. After 10 minutes of cooking, in the pan, add the soy sauce mixture and stir to combine.
7. When cooking time is complete, remove the mushrooms from oven and serve hot.

Nutrition: Calories 70 Fat 3 Carbs 15g Protein 7g

GARLIC CORN

05 minutes | 15 minutes | Fruit & Vegetables | 04 Servings

INGREDIENTS

- 2 cups corn
- 3 garlic cloves, minced
- 1 tablespoon olive oil
- Juice of 1 lime
- 1 teaspoon sweet paprika
- Salt and black pepper to the taste
- 2 tablespoons dill, chopped

COOKING STEPS

1. Mix the corn with the garlic and the other ingredients in a pan that fits the air fryer, toss, put the pan in the machine and cook at 390° f for 15 minutes.

2. Divide everything between plates and serve.

Nutrition: Calories 80 Fat 3 Carbs 9 Protein 6

Pasta & Rice

PESTO FARFALLE WITH CHERRY TOMATOES

05 minutes | 08 to 09 minutes | Pasta & Rice | 02 to 04 Servings

INGREDIENTS

- 1½ cup farfalle
- cups water
- ¾ cup vegan pesto sauce
- 1 cup cherry tomatoes, quartered

COOKING STEPS

1. Place the farfalle and water in your Instant Pot.
2. Secure the lid and cook for 7 minutes at High Pressure.
3. Once cooking is complete, do a quick pressure release. Carefully remove the lid.
4. Drain the pasta and transfer it back to the pot.
5. Stir in the sauce.
6. Press the Sauté button on your Instant Pot and cook for 1 to 2 minutes.
7. Add in the tomatoes and stir to combine.
8. Transfer to a serving dish and serve immediately.

Nutrition: Calories 370 Fat 12g Carb 45g Protein 12g

LEMONY PARMESAN RISOTTO WITH PEAS

10 minutes | 15 minutes | Pasta & Rice | 04 Servings

INGREDIENTS

- 1 tablespoon extra-virgin olive oil
- 2 tablespoons vegan butter, divided
- 1 yellow onion, chopped
- 1½ cups Arborio rice
- 2 tablespoons lemon juice
- 3½ cups chicken stock, divided
- 1½ cups frozen peas, thawed
- 2 tablespoons parsley, finely chopped
- 2 tablespoons vegan parmesan, finely grated
- 1 teaspoon grated lemon zest
- Salt and ground black pepper, to taste

COOKING STEPS

1. Press the Sauté button on your Instant Pot. Add and heat the oil and 1 tablespoon of butter.
2. Put onion and cook for 5 minutes, stirring occasionally. Mix in the rice and cook for an additional 3 minutes, stirring occasionally.
3. Stir in the lemon juice and 3 cups of stock.
4. Lock the lid. Select the Manual function and set the cooking time for 5 minutes at High Pressure.
5. Once cooking is complete, do a quick pressure release. Carefully open the lid.
6. Select the Sauté function again. Fold in the remaining ½ cup of stock and the peas and sauté for 2 minutes.
7. Add the remaining 1 tablespoon of butter, parsley, parmesan, lemon zest, salt, and pepper and stir well. Serve.

Nutrition: Calories 317 Fat 5g Carb 54g Protein 11g

RICE BOWL WITH RAISINS AND ALMONDS

| 05 minutes | 20 minutes | Pasta & Rice | 04 Servings |

INGREDIENTS

- 1 cup brown rice
- 1 cup water
- 1 cup coconut milk
- ½ cup coconut chips
- ½ cup maple syrup
- ¼ cup raisins
- ¼ cup almonds
- A pinch of cinnamon powder
  Salt, to taste

COOKING STEPS

1. Place the rice and water into the Instant Pot and give a stir.
2. Set the cooking time for 15 minutes at High Pressure and secure the lid.
3. When the timer beeps, perform a quick pressure release. Carefully remove the lid.
4. Stir in the coconut milk, coconut chips, maple syrup, raisins, almonds, cinnamon powder, and salt.
5. Lock the lid and set the cooking time for 5 minutes at High Pressure.
6. 6.Once cooking is complete, do a quick pressure release. Open the lid.
7. Serve warm.

Nutrition: Calories 261 Fat 6g Carbs 45g Protein 6g

Pasta & Rice

VEGETABLE BASMATI RICE

10 minutes | **09 to 10 minutes** | **Pasta & Rice** | **06 to 08 Servings**

INGREDIENTS

- tablespoons olive oil
- 3 cloves garlic, minced
- 1 large onion, finely chopped
- 3 tablespoons chopped cilantro stalks
- 1 cup garden peas, frozen
- 1 cup sweet corn, frozen
- 2 cups basmati rice, rinsed
- 1 teaspoon turmeric powder
- ¼ teaspoon salt
- 3 cups chicken stock
- 2 tablespoons vegan butter (optional)

COOKING STEPS

1. Press the Sauté button on the Instant Pot and heat the olive oil.
2. Add the garlic, onion, and cilantro and sauté for 5 to 6 minutes, stirring occasionally, or until the garlic is fragrant.
3. Stir in the peas, sweet corn, and rice. Scatter with the turmeric and salt. Put in the chicken stock and stir to combine.
4. Cook for 4 minutes at High Pressure.
5. Once cooking is complete, do a quick pressure release. Carefully open the lid.
6. You can add the butter, if desired. Serve warm.

Nutrition: Calories 210 Fat 0g Carbs 48g Protein 4g

STICK OF BUTTER RICE

05 minutes | **24 minutes** | **Pasta & Rice** | **04 to 06 Servings**

INGREDIENTS

- 1 stick (½ cup) vegan butter
- 2 cups brown rice
- 1½ cups French onion soup
- 1 cups vegetable stock

COOKING STEPS

1. Set your Instant Pot to Sauté and melt the butter.
2. Add the rice, onion soup, and vegetable stock to the Instant Pot and stir until combined.
3. Lock the lid and cook 22 minutes at High Pressure.
4. When the timer beeps, perform a natural pressure release for 10 minutes, then release any remaining pressure. Carefully remove the lid.
5. Serve warm.

Nutrition: Calories 390 Fat 23g Carbs 39g Protein 4g

JASMINE RICE WITH CAULIFLOWER AND PINEAPPLE

05 minutes | **20 minutes** | **Pasta & Rice** | **04 to 06 Servings**

INGREDIENTS

- cups water
- 2 cups jasmine rice
- 1 cauliflower, florets separated and chopped
- ½ pineapple, peeled and chopped
- 2 teaspoons extra virgin olive oil
- Salt and ground black pepper, to taste

COOKING STEPS

1. Stir together all the ingredients in the Instant Pot.
2. Make sure to lock the lid and cook for 20 minutes at Low Pressure.
3. When the timer beeps, perform a natural pressure release for 10 minutes, then release any remaining pressure. Carefully remove the lid.
4. Fluff with the rice spatula or fork, then serve.

Nutrition: Calories 106 Fat 1g Carbs 21g Protein 3g

Bread

SUNFLOWER SEEDS BREAD

15 minutes | 18 minutes | Bread | 04 Servings

INGREDIENTS

- 2/3 cup whole-wheat flour
- 2/3 cup plain flour
- 1/3 cup sunflower seeds
- ½ sachet instant yeast
- 1 teaspoon salt
- 2/3-1 cup lukewarm water

COOKING STEPS

1. In a bowl, mix the flours, sunflower seeds, yeast, and salt.
2. Slowly, add in the water, stirring continuously until a soft dough ball form.
3. Now, move the dough onto a lightly floured surface and knead for about 5 minutes using your hands.
4. Make a ball from the dough and place into a bowl.
5. With a plastic wrap, cover the bowl and place at a warm place for about 30 minutes.
6. Set the temperature of air fryer to 390°f. Grease a cake pan. (6"x 3")
7. Coat the top of dough with water and place into the prepared cake pan.
8. Arrange the cake pan into an air fryer basket.
9. Air fry for about 18 minutes or until a toothpick inserted in the center comes out clean.
10. Remove from air fryer and place the pan onto a wire rack for about 10-15 minutes.
11. Carefully, take out the bread from pan and put onto a wire rack until it is completely cool before slicing.
12. Cut the bread into desired size slices and serve.

Nutrition: Calories: 177 Fat 4 g Carbs 33 g Protein 5 g

BAGUETTE BREAD

15 minutes | **20 minutes** | **Bread** | **08 Servings**

INGREDIENTS

- ¾ cup warm water
- ¾ teaspoon quick yeast
- ½ teaspoon demerara sugar
- 1 cup bread flour
- ½ cup whole-wheat flour
- ½ cup oat flour
- 1¼ teaspoons salt

COOKING STEPS

1. In a large bowl, place the water and sprinkle with yeast and sugar.
2. Set aside for 5 minutes or until foamy.
3. Add the bread flour and salt mix until a stiff dough form.
4. Put the dough onto a floured surface and with your hands, knead until smooth and elastic.
5. Now, shape the dough into a ball.
6. Place the dough into a slightly oiled bowl and turn to coat well.
7. With a plastic wrap, cover the bowl and place in a warm place for about 1 hour or until doubled in size.
8. With your hands, punch down the dough and form into a long slender loaf.
9. Place the loaf onto a lightly greased baking sheet and set aside in warm place, uncovered, for about 30 minutes.
10. Press "power button" of air fry oven and turn the dial to select the "air bake" mode.
11. Press the "time button" and again turn the dial to set the cooking time to 20 minutes.
12. Now push the "temp button" and rotate the dial to set the temperature at 450°f.
13. Press "start/pause" button to start.
14. When the unit beeps to show that it's preheated, open the lid.
15. Carefully, arrange the dough onto the "wire rack" and insert in the oven.
16. Carefully, invert the bread onto wire rack to cool completely before slicing.
17. Cut the bread into desired-sized slices and serve.

Nutrition: Calories: 114 Fat 8g Carbs 28g Protein 8 g

Dessert

GRILLED SPICED FRUIT

10 minutes | **03 to 05 minutes** | **Dessert** | **04 Servings**

INGREDIENTS

- 2 peaches, peeled, pitted, and thickly sliced
- 3 plums, halved and pitted
- 3 nectarines, halved and pitted
- 1 tablespoon stevia
- ½ teaspoon ground cinnamon
- ¼ teaspoon ground allspice

COOKING STEPS

1. Pinch cayenne pepper
2. Thread the fruit, alternating the types, onto 8 bamboo or metal skewers that fit into the air fryer.
3. In a small bowl, stir together the stevia, cinnamon, allspice, and cayenne. Brush the glaze onto the fruit.
4. Grill the skewers for 3 to 5 minutes, or until lightly browned and caramelized. Cool for 5 minutes and serve.

Nutrition Calories 121 Fat 1g Carbs 30g Protein: 3g

Dessert

CARAMELIZED PEACHES WITH BLUEBERRIES

| 10 minutes | 07 to 11 minutes | Dessert | 06 Servings |

INGREDIENTS

- 6 peaches
- 100g blueberries
- 3 tbsp brown sugar
- 4 tbsp vegan yogurt
- 2 tsp cinnamon
- 2 tsp vanilla

COOKING STEPS

1. Place the peaches, cut side up, in the air fryer basket. Sprinkle evenly with the brown sugar. Bake for 7 to 11 -minutes, or until they start to brown around the edges and become tender.

2. Meanwhile, in a small bowl, stir together the yogurt, vanilla, and cinnamon.

3. When the peaches are done, transfer them to a serving plate. Top with the yogurt mixture and the blueberries. Serve immediately.

Nutrition Calories 98 Fat 1g Carbs 20g Protein 5g

STUFFED APPLES

13 minutes | **12 to 17 minutes** | **Dessert** | **04 Servings**

INGREDIENTS

- 4 medium apples, rinsed and patted dry
- 2 tablespoons freshly squeezed lemon juice
- ¼ cup golden raisins
- 3 tablespoons chopped walnuts
- 3 tablespoons dried cranberries
- 2 tablespoons packed brown sugar
- ⅓ cup apple cider

COOKING STEPS

1. Cut a strip of peel from the top of each apple and remove the core, being careful not to cut through the bottom of the apple. Sprinkle the cut parts of the apples with lemon juice and place in a 6by2inch pan.

2. In a small bowl, stir together the raisins, walnuts, cranberries, and brown sugar. Stuff one fourth of this mixture into each apple.

3. Pour the apple cider around the apples in the pan.

4. Bake in the air fryer for 12 to 17 minutes, or until the apples are tender when pierced with a fork. Serve immediately.

Nutrition Calories 122 Fat 4g Carb 22g Protein 11g

APPLE PEACH CRISP

10 minutes | **10 to 12 minutes** | **Dessert** | **04 Servings**

INGREDIENTS

- 1 apple, peeled and chopped
- 2 peaches, peeled, pitted, and chopped
- 2 tablespoons stevia
- ½ cup quick cooking oatmeal
- ⅓ cup vegan whole-wheat pastry flour
- 3 tablespoons packed brown sugar
- 2 tablespoons unsalted vegan butter, at room temperature
- ½ teaspoon ground cinnamon

COOKING STEPS

1. in a 6by2inch pan, thoroughly mix the apple, peaches, and stevia.

2. in a medium bowl, stir together the oatmeal, pastry flour, brown sugar, butter, and cinnamon until crumbly. Sprinkle this mixture over the fruit.

3. bake for 10 to 12 minutes, or until the fruit is bubbly and the topping is golden brown. Serve warm.

Nutrition calories: 237; fat: 7g (26% calories from fat; saturated fat: 4g; protein: 3g; carbohydrates: 44g; sodium: 1mg; fiber: 5g;

LENTILS AND DATES BROWNIES WITH STEVIA AND BANANA FLAVOR

10 minutes | **15 minutes** | **Dessert** | **08 Servings**

INGREDIENTS

- Canned lentils rinsed and drained 28 ounces.
- Dates 12
- 1 tbsp. Stevia
- Banana, peeled and chopped 1
- Baking soda ½ tsp.
- Almond butter 4 tbsp.
- Cocoa powder 2 tbsp.

COOKING STEPS

1. In a container of your food processor, add lentils, butter, banana, cocoa, baking soda, stevia and blend it really well.

2. In it then add some dates, some more pulse before pouring it into a greased pan that fits your air fryer and spread evenly. Now bring it to fryer and let it bake for 15 minutes at 360°f.

3. After it's done, take the brownies mix out of the oven and let it cool.

4. Lastly, cut them into pieces before arranging them on a platter to serve.

Nutrition: Calories 162 Fat 4 Carb 13 Protein 18

WALNUT AND RAISIN STUFFED APPLES

05 minutes | 20 minutes | Dessert | 02 Servings

INGREDIENTS

- 3 tablespoons crushed walnuts
- 2 tablespoons raisins
- 2 granny smith apples, cored, bottom intact
- 1 teaspoon cinnamon
- From the cupboard:
- 3 tablespoons sugar
- 2 tablespoons vegan butter, under room temperature

COOKING STEPS

1. Preheat air fryer to 350°f (180°c). Spritz the air fryer basket with cooking spray.
2. Combine all the ingredients, except for the apples, in a bowl. Stir to mix well.
3. Place the apples in the air fryer basket, bottom side down, then spoon the mixture in the core hollows of the apples.
4. Cook for 20 minutes or until the apples are wilted. Serve warm.

Nutrition Calories 322 Fat 18g Carb 33 Protein 7g

STEVIA AND PEANUT BUTTER BANANA TOAST

09 minutes | 10 minutes | Dessert | 04 Servings

INGREDIENTS

- 4 slices white bread
- 4 tablespoons peanut butter
- 2 bananas, peeled and thinly sliced
- 1 teaspoon ground cinnamon
- 3 tablespoons stevia
- From the cupboard:
- 2 tablespoons vegan butter, softened

COOKING STEPS

1. Preheat the air fryer to 375°f (190°c).

2. On a clean work surface, coat the bottom side of a slice of bread with ½ tablespoon of butter, then smear 1 tablespoon of peanut butter on top of the bread with a knife.

3. Arrange the slices of half of a banana on peanut butter. Sprinkle with ¼ teaspoon of cinnamon and drizzle with 1 tablespoon of stevia. Repeat with the remaining ingredients.

4. Arrange them in the preheated air fryer and cook for 5 minutes, then increase the temperature to 400°f (205°c) and cook for 4 more minutes or until the bread is toast and the banana slices are golden brown. You may need to work in batches to avoid overcrowding.

5. Serve the banana toast on a plate warm.

Tip: you can cut the bread slices in half to make it easier to fit the air fryer basket.

Nutrition Calories 330 Fat 16g Carb 41g Protein 6g

Dessert

BANANA S'MORES

10 minutes | **06 minutes** | **Dessert** | **04 Servings**

INGREDIENTS

- 4 unpeeled bananas
- 3 tablespoons mini marshmallows
- 3 tablespoons graham cracker cereal
- 3 tablespoons mini peanut butter chips
- 3 tablespoons mini semisweet chocolate chips

COOKING STEPS

1. Preheat the air fryer to 400°f (205°c). Spitz the air fryer basket with cooking spray.
2. Slice into the skin and meat of bananas lengthwise along the inside of the curve, keep the bottom of the skin intact.
3. Open the bananas to form pockets, then fill the pockets with remaining ingredients. Press them in bananas to avoid leaking.
4. Arrange the bananas in the preheated air fryer and cook for 6 minutes or until the bananas are soft and the skin is charred.
5. Gently remove the bananas from the air fryer basket with tongs. Allow to cool for a few minutes before serving.

Tip: arrange the bananas on the side of the air fryer basket to keep them upright with the filling facing up.

Nutrition Calories 213 Fat 5g Carbs 48g Protein 3g

Dessert

EASY CINNAMON TWISTS

| 10 minutes | 10 to 20 minutes | Dessert | 09 Servings |

INGREDIENTS

- 1 sheet vegan puff pastry, cut into 18 strips
- 1 teaspoon ground cinnamon
- From the cupboard:
- ¼ cup granulated sugar

COOKING STEPS

1. Preheat the air fryer to 330°f (166°c). Spritz the air fryer basket with cooking spray.

2. Form the puff pastry strips into twists, then put the twists in the air fryer basket. You need to work in batches to avoid overcrowding.

3. Cook for 4 minutes or until lightly browned. Flip the twists halfway through the cooking time.

4. Meanwhile, mix the cinnamon and sugar in a bowl.

5. Transfer the cooked twists in the bowl of cinnamon mixture with tongs. Allow to cool for 5 minutes, then toss to coat well and serve.

Tip: you can baste the twists with chocolate glaze for a better palate.

Nutrition Calories 99 Fat 15g Carbs 10g Protein: 0g

ORANGE CAKE

10 minutes | **23 minutes** | **Dessert** | **08 Servings**

INGREDIENTS

- Nonstick baking spray with flour
- 1¼ cups all-purpose flour
- 1/3 cup yellow cornmeal
- ¾ cup white sugar
- 1 teaspoon baking soda
- ¼ cup safflower oil
- 1¼ cups orange juice, divided
- 1 teaspoon vanilla
- ¼ cup powdered sugar

COOKING STEPS

1. Preheat the air fryer to 350°F (177°C).

2. Put flour, cornmeal, sugar, baking soda, safflower oil, 1 cup of the orange juice, and vanilla in a bowl and mix well.

3. Pour the batter into the baking pan and place in the air fryer. Bake for 23 minutes or until a toothpick inserted in the center of the cake comes out clean.

4. Remove the cake from the basket and place on a cooling rack. Using a toothpick, make about 20 holes in the cake.

5. In a small bowl, combine remaining 1/4 cup of orange juice and the powdered sugar and stir well. Drizzle this mixture over the hot cake slowly so the cake absorbs it.

Nutrition: Calories 198 Fat 10g Carb 27g Protein 1g

TAHINI OATMEAL CHOCOLATE CHUNK COOKIES

10 minutes | 15 minutes | Dessert | 08 Servings

INGREDIENTS

- 1/3 cup of tahini
- 1/4 cup of walnuts
- 1/4 cup of maple syrup
- 1/4 cup of Chocolate chunks
- 1/4 tsp of sea salt
- 2 tablespoons of almond flour
- 1 teaspoon of vanilla, it is optional
- 1 cup of gluten free oat flakes
- 1 teaspoon of cinnamon, it is optional

COOKING STEPS

1. Let the air fryer Preheat to 350° F.
2. In a big bowl, add the maple syrup, cinnamon if used, the tahini, salt, and vanilla if used. Mix well, then add in the walnuts, oat flakes, and almond meal. Then fold the chocolate chips gently.
3. Now the mix is ready, take a full tablespoon of mixture, separate into eight amounts. Wet clean damp hands press them on a baking tray or with a spatula.
4. Place four cookies, or more depending on your air fryer size, line the air fryer basket with parchment paper in one single layer.
5. Let them cook for 56 minutes at 350° f, air fry for more minutes if you like them crispy.

Nutrition: calories: 185 Fat 12g Carb 15g Protein 15g

CHOCOLATE BANANA PACKETS

5 minutes | **15 minutes** | **Dessert** | **01 Servings**

INGREDIENTS

- Miniature marshmallows 2 tablespoons
- Cereal, cinnamon, crunchy, slightly crushed 2 tablespoons
- Banana, peeled 1 piece
- Chocolate chips, semi-sweet 2 tablespoons

COOKING STEPS

1. Preheat air fryer to 390 °F.
2. Slightly open banana by cutting lengthwise. Place on sheet of foil.
3. Fill sliced banana with chocolate chips and marshmallows. Close foil packet.
4. Air-fry for fifteen to twenty minutes.
5. Open packet and top banana with crushed cereal.

Nutrition: Calories 270 fat 2g Carbs 50 g Protein 0g

GRANOLA COOKIES

10 minutes | 15 minutes | Dessert | 30 Servings

INGREDIENTS

- ½ cup caster sugar
- ½ cup cooking oil
- ½ cup ground almonds
- 2 cups plain flour
- 1 teaspoon baking powder
- 1 teaspoon baking soda
- ¼ cup granola

COOKING STEPS

1. Preheat the air fryer to 275°f/140°c.
2. Mix together the caster sugar, cooking oil and ground almonds in a stand mixer.
3. Mix together flour, baking powder and baking soda and gradually add to the ground almond mixture.
4. Fold in the granola.
5. Line the air fryer basket and air fryer double layer rack with parchment paper. Drop teaspoon full of batter onto the parchment papers.
6. Set the timer for 15 minutes.
7. Allow the cookies to cool in the air fryer for a few minutes before transferring to a serving plate.
8. Serve and enjoy!

Nutrition: Calories 133 Fat 2 Carbs 13 Protein 8

FIGS AND COCONUT BUTTER MIX

06 minutes | 04 minutes | Dessert | 03 Servings

INGREDIENTS

- 2 tablespoons coconut butter
- figs, halved
- ¼ cup sugar
- 1 cup almond, toasted and chopped

COOKING STEPS

1. Put butter in a pan that fits your air fryer and melt over medium high heat.
2. Add figs, sugar and almonds, toss, introduce in your air fryer and cook at 300 ° for 4 minutes.
3. Divide into bowls and serve cold.
4. Enjoy!

Nutrition: Calories 170 Fat 4 Carbs 7 Protein 9

CINNAMON TOAST

05 minutes | 05 minutes | Dessert | 06 Servings

INGREDIENTS

- 2 tsp. pepper
- 1 ½ tsp. vanilla extract
- 1 ½ tsp. cinnamon
- ½ C. sweetener of choice
- 1 C. coconut oil
- slices whole wheat bread

COOKING STEPS

1. Melt coconut oil and mix with sweetener until dissolved. Mix in remaining ingredients minus bread till incorporated.
2. Spread mixture onto bread, covering all area.
3. Place coated pieces of bread in your Air fryer.
4. Cook 5 minutes at 400°F. Remove and cut diagonally. Enjoy.

Nutrition: Calories 124 Fat 12g Carb 10g Protein 3g

APPLE DUMPLINGS

10 minutes | **25 minutes** | **Dessert** | **04 Servings**

INGREDIENTS

- 2 tbsp. melted coconut oil
- 2 puff vegan pastry sheets
- 1 tbsp. brown sugar
- 2 tbsp. raisins
- 2 small apples of choice

COOKING STEPS

1. Ensure your air fryer is preheated to 356°F.
2. Core and peel apples and mix with raisins and sugar.
3. Place a bit of apple mixture into puff pastry sheets and brush sides with melted coconut oil.
4. Place into the Air fryer. Cook 25 minutes, turning halfway through. Will be golden when done.

Nutrition: Calories 163 Fat 9g Carbs 21g Protein 1g

COCOA AND ALMONDS BARS

30 minutes | 04 minutes | Dessert | 06 Servings

INGREDIENTS

- ¼ cup cocoa nibs
- 1 cup almonds, drenched and depleted
- 2 tablespoons cocoa powder
- ¼ cup hemp seeds
- ¼ cup goji berries
- ¼ cup coconut, destroyed
- dates, hollowed and drenched

COOKING STEPS

1. Put almonds in your food processor, mix, include hemp seeds, cocoa nibs, cocoa powder, goji, coconut and mix quite well.

2. Add dates, mix well once more, spread on a lined heating sheet that accommodates the air fryer cooker and cook at 320 °F for about 4 minutes.

3. Cut into two halves and keep in the cooler for 30 minutes before serving.

4. Enjoy the recipe!

Nutrition: Calories 140 Fat 6 Fiber 3 Carbs 7 Protein 19

Dessert

CASHEW BARS

10 minutes | 15 minutes | Dessert | 06 Servings

INGREDIENTS

- 1/3 cup stevia
- ¼ cup almond meal
- 1 tablespoon almond spread
- 1 and ½ cups cashews, hacked
- dates, slashed
- ¾ cup coconut, destroyed
- 1 tablespoon chia seeds

COOKING STEPS

1. In a bowl, blend stevia in with almond meal and almond spread and mix well.
2. Add cashews, coconut, dates and chia seeds and mix well once more.
3. Spread this on a lined heating sheet that accommodates the air fryer cooker and press well.
4. Introduce in the fryer and cook at 300°F for about 15 minutes.
5. Leave blend to chill off, cut into medium bars and serve. Enjoy!

Nutrition: Calories 121 Fat 4 Carb 5 Protein 6

Dessert

Dessert

Printed in Great Britain
by Amazon